The New IDIOMS IN ACTION

George Reeves

HEINLE & HEINLE PUBLISHERS
A Division of Wadsworth, Inc.
Boston, Massachusetts 02116

Library of Congress Cataloging in Publication Data

Reeves, George, 1929–
The new idioms in action.

Includes index.
1. English language--Text-books for foreign speakers. 2. English language--Idioms. I. Title.
PE1128.R433 1985 428.3'4 85-5102
ISBN 0-88377-301-5

Printed in the U.S.A.

First printing: October 1985
11 12 13 14 15 16 17

To Ingrid and Jan Romare, Good Friends

PREFACE

Idiomatic English is real English. It's the English that English-speaking people normally use. It's the blood and guts of their language.

That's why ESL and EFL students must learn it. That's why they must experience idioms and use idioms—hear them, say them, write them.

The next step is more complicated. They need to learn how idioms "fit" spoken and written language. They need to see links between situation and structure. They need to understand the unity between human interaction and words, culture, and grammar.

Finally, to make "real-people English" theirs, students must feel caught up in getting it. That is why my idioms appear in contexts that not only inform and amuse but—more important—implicate students' deeper interests and values. That is why my dialogs tell of a love-hate relationship between a man and a woman of different background, nationality, and race. That is why national pride, cultural preconceptions, and problems of race and sex challenge students on every page. That is why customs, values, and beliefs—of peoples everywhere—permeate the idiom-learning process. That is why idioms appear not as merely useful but as expressive of our human condition.

ACKNOWLEDGMENTS

In revising the original *Idioms in Action*, I turned it into a different book. Earl Stevick must bear blame: His landmark *Memory, Meaning, and Method* (Newbury House Publishers, 1976) made me want to relate language to the whole student—head, heart, and funnybone. Simon, Howe, and Kirschenbaum's *Values Clarification* (Hart Publishing Company, 1977) suggested how to do it. ("The Alligator River Story," at the end of **Sex-Mad Americans**, comes from them.) Of course, how can I forget Sue Marsick, who first interested me in values clarification and whose "Three Telegrams" ends **Heart Attacks: The American Way of Death**. I especially wish to thank Anne Dow, director of the EFL program at Harvard University, for her permission to teach there an earlier version of *The New Idioms*. Nor can I forget Suzanne Griffin, whose thorough, thoughtful comments helped me more than I care to admit, or Judy E. Winn-Bell Olsen (The Alemany Press) who graciously let me use seven of her idiom games, all of them *Communication-Starters*. Finally, I owe much to Professor Norman Prange, friend, colleague, grammarian.

As for the python and its sinister master who slither and slink their way through this book—they are the creations of a superb cartoonist. Jan Romare, thank you.

Final thanks go, of course, to my typist Carolyn Olszewski, who came through . . . beautifully.

TO THE TEACHER

Levels of Use—TOEFL 425–500.
TOEFL 500–550.

How the Book Works

What is the aim of each lesson? **The Spoken and Written Mastery of Idioms in a Variety of Contexts.**

How is it achieved? By two preparatory and six applicatory exercises, each of which challenges students with a particular language activity:

ROLE PLAYING, the first exercise, contextualizes five idioms in a short, provocative dialog. Students infer the meanings of the idioms from it.

LESSON 5: ARE AMERICANS IMPOLITE?

Mimi **On the whole**, Americans aren't polite. Most of them have bad manners.

Sam I don't believe it!

Mimi Well, what do you **think of** strangers who call you by your first name? On Wednesday I moved into my apartment. On Thursday the janitor came to fix the heating. **Right away** he called me Anne-Marie. The next day the postman called me Annie. **In fact**, two minutes after they meet me, Americans use my first name.

Sam But it's an American custom. They only mean to be friendly.

Mimi We **are used to** politeness in France.

Sam But customs are different in your country. That's why some American tourists **think of** the French as unfriendly.

Mimi They're idiots!

IDIOM CHECK then defines each idiom and gives examples, synonyms, antonyms, and constraints—lexical, grammatical, sociolinguistic.

in fact Really; in reality; actually—often used emphatically.

Hitler isn't dead. In fact, he's alive and living in Paraguay.
Mimi didn't believe Sam. In fact, she called him a liar.

Equivalent: **in point of fact.**

be used to Be accustomed to; have the habit of + ING.

John is used to smokING cigars.
For many years Henry walked in his sleep. His wife was used to it.

Contrast: **used to** (Lesson 13).

SPELLING, the third exercise, supplies paragraph-length contexts. The no-error format guides students to good grammar and correct spelling.

Directions: Write (or say) the appropriate idiom. Use one letter for each blank.

get up • at first • ahead of time • get on (someone's) nerves • of course

tense

Mimi makes mistakes on idioms and becomes angry. Idioms g/e/t

person

o/n h/e/r n/e/r/v/e/s, so she leaves bed early to study them.

person

She even g/e/t/s u/p at 5:00 a.m. O/f c/o/u/r/s/e,

she is never late with her ESL homework. She always finishes it a/h/e/a/d o/f t/i/m/e.

A/t f/i/r/s/t Mimi didn't do too well in Professor Smith's ESL class, but after a few weeks she got A's on her idiom tests.

SUBSTITUTING calls for replacing the capitalized words with their idiomatic equivalent and recopying the sentence correctly. It aims to cue, channel, and sharpen idiom comprehension.

Sam **left his bed** late today. Sam got up late today.

CHOOSING requires just that: choosing the idiom appropriate to the context by means of lexical and syntactical clues.

At first Mimi came to English class ahead of time, but now she's always late.

COMPLETING asks students to select the appropriate idiom, as in **choosing**. They must then use their own words to *complete the context*, thus preparing themselves for the freer idiomatic writing and speaking which follows.

My boyfriend could do two things at the same time. He could drive a car and watch the pretty girls walk by.

UPPER INTERMEDIATE

CONTEXTUALIZING, with six to ten interrelated sentences, provides enough ideas for a short talk or for one to two idiomatic paragraphs. Without having to worry about where their next idea is coming from, students can concentrate on how best—*in their own words*—to contextualize their idioms.

1) John didn't like his job; it made him nervous. 2) His boss was angry with him. 3) He said to John, "Come to work early." 4) John didn't listen. 5) Every morning he slept later and later. 6) He was always late to work. 7) His boss fired him.

Students might say or write something like this:

Why didn't John GET UP *earlier?* OF COURSE, *he had his reasons: He didn't like his job; it* GOT ON HIS NERVES. AT FIRST *his boss only warned him about being late to work. A few weeks later he fired him.*

I agree with John. Who likes to GET UP *and go to work every morning? No one. Who arrives* AHEAD OF TIME? *Only the boss.*

VALUING, the final exercise, encourages students to write about, speak about, and compare American culture with their own. It does this by having them act as judges or as participants in a culturally ambiguous situation. It also ties in with **role playing** so as to keep newly acquired idioms "on stage." For example, the situation described below—connected by subject with the dialog **Are Americans Impolite**—enlarges upon Mimi and Sam's discussion of first names:

Discuss (write about) your choice, using the idioms you have just learned.

Your ESL teacher is a 35-year-old woman, Mrs. Jane Smith. She asks you to call her Jane. How do you feel about her request?

1. I feel that she wants to be my friend and I use her first name freely.
2. I know that she wants me to relax, but I feel uneasy when I call her Jane.
3. I rarely use her name.
4. I don't call her any name at all.
5. I continue to call her "Mrs. Smith."

Student and teacher might interact like this:

Ms. Wong In my previous English class, I had a similar problem: my teacher wanted us to use her first name. I was surprised. **In fact**, I was shocked. In China we **think of** our teacher as a superior person. It would be impolite to use her first name.

Teacher How did you solve your problem?

Ms. Wong I didn't call her by any name.

Teacher But why didn't you call her "Mrs." and her last name?

Ms. Wong What if she got angry at me for not doing what she asked?

Teacher I understand your feelings.

Ms. Wong Many Americans use people's first names **right away.** **On the whole**, Americans are very informal compared with us Chinese. Even though I know this, **I am used to** my own customs and it's difficult to . . .

Teacher I understand. Now tell me—in China were there persons who called *you* by your first name but expected you to call *them* by their formal name?

Ms. Wong Yes . . . etc.

Suggestions to Make Your Life Easier

1. Have your students do their **sample lesson** in class. Check that they follow directions and finish each exercise correctly. (*Cuts down on future student errors.*)

2. Even if you assign an idiom lesson for homework, always read aloud **Role Playing**. Then read it again, asking your students to repeat each sentence after you. Better yet, assign students to role-play it. (*Result: Gets students started on their homework.*)

3. If time permits, discuss **Idiom Check**. Urge students to refer to it while they do their exercises. (*Cuts down on errors.*)

4. On written work students can profitably correct their own mistakes in **Spelling, Substituting**, and **Choosing**. Simply read the correct version aloud to them *before* you collect their lessons. (*No need to be a robot corrector.*)

5. PEER-GROUP TEACHING: The first three or four times your class does **Completing** and **Contextualizing**, group students into twos or threes and let each group work out a common answer to be given orally or written on the chalkboard. (*Builds confidence in intermediates.*)

6. For lower intermediate students, do **Valuing** orally in peer groups. (*Resist temptation: Except for grammatical corrections, STAY OUT of the discussions.*)

7. For you "comp" teachers who want your students to get in some oral idiom practice, here's a useful way: With student books open, read **Role Playing**. Students close their books and you reread, stopping at each place an idiom appears. Ask which idiom. THEN, with everyone helping, have students produce the entire sentence, idiom included. And so on. (*Time required: 10 to 15 minutes.*)

8. **Idiom Review Exercises** help students to sharpen their recall and comprehension for upcoming tests.

9. BILEVEL TEAROUT TESTS every three lessons let you monitor student progress.

10. Contractions and ellipses permeate real-life conversations *and* **Role Playing**. So familiarize your students right away with CONTRACTIONS (see page 184) and ELLIPTICAL CONSTRUCTIONS (see page 185).

11. LOG SHEET OF IDIOMATIC ENGLISH. Ask your students to keep a "log" of what they're hearing and what they're saying outside ESL class. The better they keep their log, the more real English becomes to them. (See page 195.)

12. Students write their own DIALOGS—idiomatic give-and-take on American life. They then take turns role playing. (*Videotape your students if you can.*)

13. GAMES

a. Bingo:

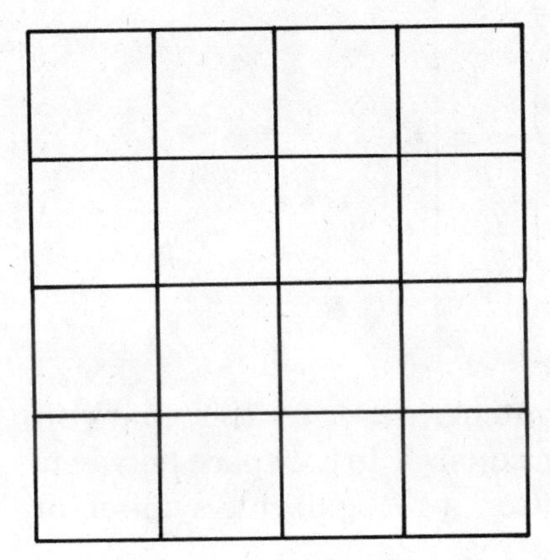

Make a ditto master of a large bingo grid with 16 or 25 squares (4 × 4 or 5 × 5) and run off copies. Pass out copies of this empty grid to your students.

Dictate 25 idioms (or a mix of idioms and other new vocabulary covered in class) to your students. They are to write the words on the grid in *random order*–that is, each grid should have the same words but in different squares. (If everybody had exactly the same order of words, everybody would get "bingo" at the same time.)

After you have dictated all the words and students have written them in their grids, you are ready to play the game. Give a *paraphrase* of each idiom or other word, either by itself or in the context of a sentence. Students must recognize the idiom from the paraphrase and mark it on their grids.

The first student to have five marks in a row (or four, if you're playing with 16-square grids) is the winner. He or she calls "bingo!" and wins a prize, such as a ballpoint pen, or a paperback.

b. Concentration:

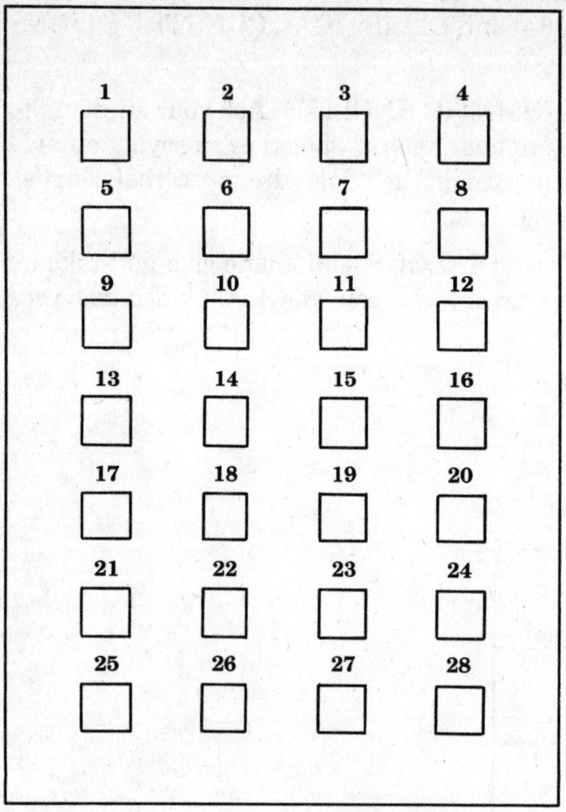

1 2 3 4
5 6 7 8
9 10 11 12
13 14 15 16
17 18 19 20
21 22 23 24
25 26 27 28

Use a large piece of paperboard or butcher paper for this. Mark off 16 or more squares, with space between squares. In the space between, mark each square with a number, a letter, a recognizable symbol, or some combination.

You will need half as many idioms as squares: that is, if you have 16 squares, choose 8 idioms; if you have 20 squares, choose 10 idioms; etc. Write these idioms, one each, on cards that will fit into the squares you have marked off on your large piece of paper. Then take an equal number of new cards and write paraphrases of these idioms on them.

Put your cards—half of them idioms, half of them paraphrases—in the squares you have marked off, in totally random order, *face down.*

Students are divided into teams. They take turns guessing which two numbers will make an idiom-definition pair. When a guess has been made, the two numbered cards are turned face up so that the class can see if they make a pair. If they *do* match, a point is given to that team and they get another turn. If the cards don't match, they are again turned face down, and the other team has a turn guessing which numbers might make a pair.

As the game progresses, students with good concentration will remember the location of idioms and paraphrases revealed during wrong guesses and will be able to match them for right guesses. Each student should have his or her own turn at guessing, but they may be prompted by other team members.

This can be a game of great excitement, hilarity, and general camaraderie, particularly with chewing gum "prizes" for all. It's a good Friday or "just-before-holiday" game.

c. Tic-Tac-Toe:

This brings much the same response as Concentration but requires somewhat more strategy and is recommended as a more "advanced" game.

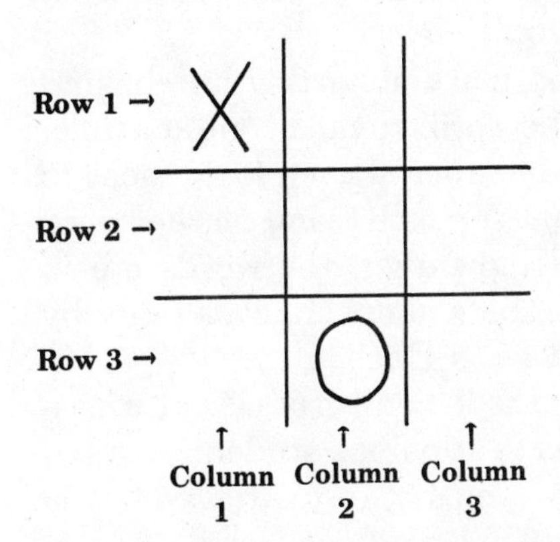

Draw a tic-tac-toe grid on the board—a large one. Mark the rows "Row 1—Row 2—Row 3" and the columns "Column 1—Column 2—Column 3." Be sure everyone can identify the squares within the grid (as in the "top row, middle column" or "row 1, column 2."

Play a regular game of tic-tac-toe with the class—them against you. They tell you where to mark their X; you mark your own O. Or have two students play but tell you where to draw the X's and O's while the class watches.

When the dynamics of the game are understood, you are ready to "plug in" the idioms. Take nine cards, each of which has the paraphrase of one idiom written on it. Put one card in each square of the tic-tac-toe grid. (You can make it harder by putting the cards face down, so students have less time to figure them out.)

Divide the class into team X and team O. Each team has only one turn to direct you, until all members have had a turn (though members of the same team can help each other).

When a team member tells you which square to mark with X or O, he or she must first correctly perform the task of that square—in this case, correctly stating the idiom when given the paraphrase. Or you might want to have the idiom on the card, and ask the student to use it correctly in a sentence. (This is harder.)

If the student performs the task correctly, remove the card and place X or O in that square.

If the student does *not* do the task correctly, it becomes the other team's turn. They may choose to work on the same square, or choose a different one.

This becomes quite exciting when several squares are marked, and there is one crucial square remaining to determine which team will get the three-in-a-row to win. I have had games where a crucial task was botched several times in succession as the turn traded back and forth between teams and the tension mounted.

The winning team, of course, is the one who first gets three X's or O's in a row.

d. Relays:

Recognition Relay: Make a list of 20 to 25 idioms, or mix idioms and other vocabulary. Then make a second list of the same words, in different order. If possible, write these two lists on the blackboard before class, or during a class break, or write them on sheets of butcher paper to tape on the board at the proper time.

Divide the class into two teams, and mark a starting line behind which they must stand. Then read out the words to them, one at a time, in random order. As you say a word, a member of each team races to that team's list (two lists, remember? one for each team) on the board and draws a line through the word. (Remember, the words are in different order on each list.) Team members may help each other by calling "up," "down," etc., but it must be in English.

The first student to find the word on the list and cross it out wins a point for his or her team. It's a good idea to appoint a student to watch closely to see who actually makes it first—you may be distracted by the enthusiasm of your class.

When you read out the next word, a new member of each team should come to the board, and so on, until all members have had their chance. If your students' motor abilities vary widely because of age or handicap, you may want to line up each team beforehand, so that you can match their abilities before the competition starts. If you have just one student whose abilities are very different from the others', you could appoint that person scorekeeper or judge of who gets each point.

Another idea, one which "tones down" this rather boisterous competition, is to have contestants walk to the board and pick up the chalk before you read the words for them to mark off.

I have described this as a two-team competition. Of course, you can have as many teams as you have patience to make lists for and attention to keep track of. More teams means more turns and more practice for each student.

Conversion Relay: Again, two teams. They take turns running up to the front, taking a slip of paper with a paraphrase, converting the paraphrase to an idiom. If one team misses (in this game, they go alternately, not simultaneously) the other gets a chance at that paraphrase, plus the next one, which is their official turn. Keep score.

Usage Relay: Same as conversion relay, but students get slips of paper with idioms and must put them into appropriate sentences.

e. Card Match-up Competition:

Students are on their feet, ready to move around. Half of them are given a card with an idiom written on it; the other half have a paraphrase or a sentence with a blank where the idiom should go.

Students must mix and find their partner with the corresponding card. You can make this a race or a sociable mixer. Good icebreaker for new classes.

TO THE STUDENT

What Is an Idiom?

Combine two or more words to say something and maybe you have an idiom. If you can't understand its meaning from its individual words, then, for sure, you have an idiom. **In time** is an idiom. So is **on time**.

Are There Different Kinds of Idioms?

There sure are. There are idioms that act like adverbs (**in time, on time**), others like verbs (**get on, get off**) and some like nouns (**run-in** as in **I had a run-in with my boss**).

Why Study Idioms That I Already Know?

Because you don't really know them. You only recognize them. For example, you probably recognize **in time** and **on time**. But can you tell the difference between them? Can you use them correctly in sentences?

No? Then it's like having a car in the garage but not knowing how to drive it.

In short, unused knowledge cannot help you. That is why *The New Idioms in Action* makes you USE, USE, USE your everyday idioms. So do its exercises carefully and soon you will—

1. Speak and write many of the most frequent (and useful) idioms in the English language.
2. Sound less like a book and more like a human being.
3. Use your English better and better.

Study Aids

1. A *Correction Guide* to help you understand and correct your idiom mistakes.
2. A *Log Sheet of Idiomatic Usage* for idioms you hear or speak outside ESL class.
3. An *Index* to tell you which lesson contains which idiom.
4. A *Lexicon* to list the meaning of each idiom, a sentence exemplifying that meaning, and sometimes a second sentence for exemplifying another frequent meaning.
5. A *List of Contractions* to help you to make your English sound natural, not stiff.
6. A *List of Elliptical Constructions* to show you how to "shorten" sentences.
7. *Idiom Review Exercises* to help you to spell your idioms correctly and understand them better. Use them just before idiom tests.
8. *Names and Nicknames* to help you and Americans to be friends.

Fun Things

1. *Colorful Sayings* come at the end of every lesson. They're just for you. Enjoy them. Laugh at them. Can you think of similar expressions in your native language?
2. *Games*. There are seven idiom games. Ask your teacher about playing them in class. What a fun way to learn!

CONTENTS

PART TWO • All Tenses (Simple and Continuous)

The New IDIOMS IN ACTION

PART ONE

Simple Past, Present, and Future Tenses (plus Present Continuous)

Sample Lesson

MIMI PRACTICES HER IDIOMS

ROLE PLAYING

Mimi When do you **get up** (1), Sam?

Sam On a bus. On a bus I always **get up** to give old people my seat.

Mimi I don't mean *stand.* I mean *leave your bed.*

Sam But which **get up** is the right **get up**? How do I know?

Mimi Don't laugh! I'm practicing idioms and I need help. Tell me, are all idioms *two-word verbs*—like **get up**?

Sam No, idioms like **at first** (2) and **ahead of time** (3) are *adverbs.*

Mimi Use **at first** and **ahead of time** in sentences. I can understand them better that way.

Sam **At first** Mimi came to English class **ahead of time**. Now she's always late.

Mimi Sam, you are **getting on my nerves** (4).

Sam **Getting on your nerves**—that's another idiom, **of course** (5).

Mimi Grrrrrrrrrrrrr.

> Here are definitions and sentences using the idioms in your dialog. Study them BEFORE you speak or write your idioms.

1. **get up*** verb a. Leave your bed. *Mimi got up at 5:00 a.m. to finish her homework.*

   Contrast: **go to bed.**

*For additional meanings of **get up**, see the Index. Warning!!! Like **get up**, many idioms have *several* meanings, but in your dialogs and exercises, you will work with only one meaning—*a.*

b. Stand; rise to your feet. *Every student in my class must get up and give a report.*

Contrast: **sit down.**

2. **at first** adverbial phrase Early; before something starts; in the beginning. *It was only a small fire at first./ At first Sam disliked Professor Smith; later he liked him.*

   Compare: **first.**

3. **ahead of time** adverbial phrase Early; before someone/something is expected. *I finished my shopping ahead of time and got home before my father did.*

   Contrast: **late.**

4. **get on**/my, your, her, his, one's, our, their/**nerves** verb phrase, intransitive. Irritate, bother, upset. *My baby makes a lot of noise. He's always getting on my nerves.*

5. **of course** adverbial phrase Naturally; certainly; what you would expect. *John lent Mary five dollars. Of course, she appreciated it.*

In each of the six exercises below, use these idioms: 1. **get up** 2. **at first** 3. **ahead of time** 4. **getting on (someone's) nerves** 5. **of course**

SPELLING

Write (or say) the appropriate idiom. Use one letter for each blank.

Example: Sam, now you *a/r/e g/e/t/t/i/n/g o/n m/y* (2d person; present continuous tense)

n/e/r/v/e/s. (Idiom 4)

Mimi and Sam try hard to learn English. It _/_/_/_ _/_ _/_/_/_/_ _/_/_/_/_/_ (Idiom 4) when they don't know the answers. So they _/_/_ _/_ (Idiom 1) early every morning to study their idioms. As a result, they always finish their homework _/_/_/_/_ _/_ _/_/_/_. (Idiom 3)

Now the two girls understand everything their teacher says and they get A's. But _/_ _/_/_/_/_ (Idiom 2) they didn't understand much English, so _/_ _/_/_/_/_/_ (Idiom 5) they got bad grades.

SUBSTITUTING

Replace boldface words with appropriate idioms. Then copy (or repeat aloud) the whole sentence in the correct tense and person.

present tense; 3rd person

Example: Sam **irritates** Mimi. *Sam gets on Mimi's nerves* ______.

1. They **irritated** us. ______.
2. **In the beginning** I didn't understand math. ______.
3. My English class began ten minutes **early** today. ______.
4. **Naturally**, I like to go to parties. ______.
5. Sam **left his bed** late yesterday. ______.

CHOOSING

Write or say the appropriate idiom.

person

Example: When Sam yelled at Mimi, he *got on her nerves* ______.

tense

I wanted to arrive at the movie theater ______ or, at the latest, for the start of the film. I told Sam he was driving in the wrong direction. A few minutes later he admitted his mistake, but ______ he didn't listen to me. This irritated me. He ______. But I didn't say anything. ______ ______, we arrived late. In my opinion, arriving late at a movie is as bad as ______ late in the morning.

COMPLETING

Supply the appropriate idiom. Then finish the sentence in your own words, using the correct tense and person.

Examples: My girlfriend didn't like me to do it. *I got on her nerves* because I *chewed my fingernails in public* ______.

She was angry. I tried hard not to *get on her nerves* because she *had a very bad temper* ______.

1. Last year my friend John ________________ because, night after night, he

_ .

2. Do you study hard? Yes, ________________ , I_ _ _ _ _ _ _ _ .

3. *Now* Sam knows the truth about Mimi, but ________________ he believed

_ .

4. If you finish your homework ________________ , you can_ _ _ _ _ _

_ .

5. Yesterday John ________________ late because_ _ _ _ _ _ _ _ .

CONTEXTUALIZING

In your own words write (or tell) a story. Include three idioms from this lesson and use the ideas below. (50 to 75 words)

1) John liked to sleep late. 2) He often came to work late. 3) This began to irritate his boss. 4) She said, "Come to work early." 5) In the following days John made an effort to be early. 6) Later he began to be late again. 7) Naturally his boss fired him.

VALUING

Discuss (write about) the questions below, using your idioms wherever you can.

Every morning Robert's wife Stella leaves her bed a few minutes before her husband does. She makes breakfast and feeds the children. Recently, Stella said to Robert: "On weekends you don't work. You ought to leave bed first and feed the children. It's only fair."

If you are a man, how do you react to Stella's request? Do you think she is right—that you don't try hard enough? Or do you tell her that breakfast and the children are her job?

If you are a woman, what is your reaction to Stella? Do women in your country act like this? Do you think that Stella is right? Wrong? Why?

____

____

____

____

____

____

____

____

____

____

ANSWERS TO THE SAMPLE LESSON

SPELLING

gets on their nerves . . . get up . . . ahead of time . . . at first . . . of course

SUBSTITUTING

1. They *got on our nerves.*
2. *At first* I didn't understand math.
3. My English class began ten minutes *ahead of time* today.
4. *Of course,* I like to go to parties.
5. Sam *got up* late yesterday.

CHOOSING

ahead of time . . . at first . . . got on my nerves . . . of course . . . getting up

COMPLETING*

1. Last year my friend John *got on my nerves* because, night after night, he *played his HiFi very loudly.*
   Last year my friend John *got on my nerves* because, night after night, he *had a party but never invited me.*
   Last year my friend John *got on my nerves* because, night after night, he *would type on a noisy electric typewriter.*
2. Do you study hard? Yes, *of course,* I *do.*
   Do you study hard? Yes, *of course,* I *study hard.*
   Do you study hard? Yes, *of course,* I *spend lots of time on all my subjects.* Etc.
3. Now Sam knows the truth about Mimi, but *at first* he believed *that she was a nice girl.*
   Now Sam knows the truth about Mimi, but *at first* he believed *that people lied about her.*
   Now Sam knows the truth about Mimi, but *at first* he believed *everything she told him about herself.* Etc.

*A few possible answers are given. Many *different* answers would be equally correct.

4. If you finish your homework *ahead of time*, you can *go to the movies.*

   If you finish your homework *ahead of time*, you can *start the next lesson.*
   If you finish your homework *ahead of time*, you can *help me with mine.* Etc.
5. Yesterday John *got up* late because *he was on vacation.*
   Yesterday John *got up* late because *his alarm clock wasn't working.*
   Yesterday John *got up* late because *his teacher was sick and there was no 8 a.m. class.* Etc.

CONTEXTUALIZING

Why did John **get on his** boss's **nerves**? Because John was always late to work. **At first** his boss only warned him. **Of course**, a few weeks later she fired him.

I agree with John. Who likes to **get up** and go to work every morning? No one. Who arrives **ahead of time**? Only the boss.

VALUING

In **Valuing** there is no right answer. Different countries follow different customs and believe in different values. So talk with your classmates from other countries. Try to learn about their values. Try to learn why they consider some actions and some kinds of work important but not others. Ask them which people in their country do what work and why? (Think of Robert and Stella.)

When you discuss Stella and Robert, remember to use your idioms. Remember, also, that these idioms can tell you about the values of American society. (Think of the many American idioms and proverbs about using time profitably.)

A student might write something like this: A year ago I became a wife. **At first** I didn't like to **get up** every morning and make breakfast for my husband. I especially didn't like to be the only person who sat down at the breakfast table **ahead of time**. That is why making breakfast for him **got on my nerves**. I understand, **of course**, that it is the custom in my country for women to do this. I don't like the custom.

TESTS

At the end of every three idiom lessons, there is a test on the fifteen idioms you have learned. This test has two levels: one for low intermediate students and the other for high intermediates.

Level I. From the **Completing exercises** of these three lessons your teacher will (at the time of your test) choose five incomplete sentences. You will do exactly as you did in the **Sample Lesson**: Write in the appropriate idiom and finish each sentence in your own words.

Example: At first Mimi disliked Sam, but later . . . **she began to love him.**

Level II.

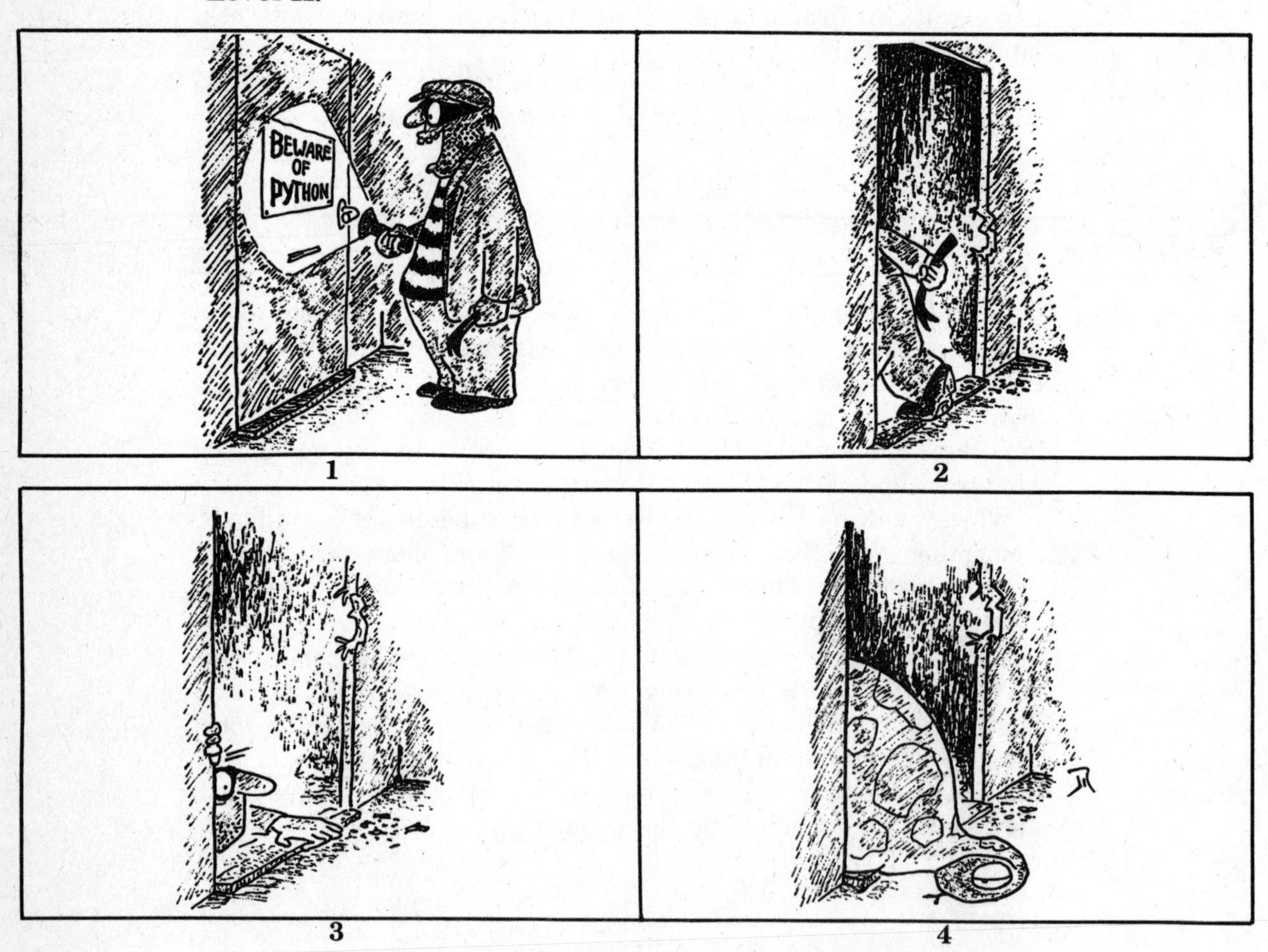

These four cartoons tell the story of a robber who met a python. In a short paragraph, write about this meeting. Include some of the idioms you have just studied in your **Sample Lesson.**

Example: The sign on the door said "BEWARE OF PYTHON!" **At first** the robber laughed at this sign. **Of course**, he didn't believe there was a big snake behind the door, so BANG! BANG! he broke open the door. But the noise **got on** the python's **nerves** and it ate him. Poor robber! He isn't laughing now.

WHO ARE MIMI AND SAM?

Mimi Bouvier

The Bouvier family lives in Paris near Notre Dame. Mimi's father sells new and used cars; her mother works for a tourist agency. She has two younger brothers.

Mimi is a high school graduate and she knows a great deal about France and French culture. For her, France is the best country in the world.

She doesn't like other countries very much.

She also believes that she is more polite, beautiful, and intelligent than other people. You may or may not agree with Mimi's opinion of herself.

Sam Yamaguchi

His mother directs an elementary school; his father teaches English at a university in Kyoto, Japan.

But in the 1960s the Yamaguchis lived in San Francisco, California. Sam was born there. This made him a second-generation Japanese-American—a *Nisei*, as the Japanese say.

When Sam was eleven, his family moved back to Japan. He later studied engineering there. Recently he decided to return to California and continue his studies at Stanford. As a graduate student, he feels that he must improve his English (which is already quite good).

Mimi + Sam

Mimi and Sam meet in Professor Smith's English class and soon become friends. Sam has never met anyone so relaxed and free as Mimi; she has never met anyone so serious and conservative as Sam.

Opposites attract, certainly. But will Sam and Mimi continue to like each other? Will fire and water unite? READ ON!

Lesson 1

GOD AND THE FRENCH

ROLE PLAYING

(In Professor Smith's ESL class, her students are introducing themselves. Sam Yamaguchi, a graduate student in engineering, is speaking. Mimi Bouvier, who wants to become a French-English translator, is waiting her turn.)

Sam . . . and my parents **went back** to Japan when I was eleven. I **came back** here only a month ago. Of course, I didn't speak much English in Japan.

Professor Smith Sam, you're going to speak a lot of English **from now on**. I'll personally **see to** it.

Sam Thank you, m'am. It will help me to re-Americanize myself. (Sits down.)

Mimi (Standing up and looking at Sam.) I'm Mimi, I'm French, and I'll *always* remain French because the French are so intelligent. You'll understand me when I tell you about God and Saint Peter.*

Professor Smith About God? About Saint Peter?

Mimi You see, one day God felt sad. When Saint Peter saw this, he asked, "**What's the matter**, God?"
"I thought something terrible," God said. "In ten thousand years all the French will be dead."
"So????"
"So then there will be nobody left on earth who will be able to understand me."

Professor Smith I wonder who told Mimi that story?

Sam God.

*Saint Peter—in Roman Catholicism, the Chief Angel of God. As are most French, Mimi is Catholic.

IDIOM CHECK

go back Return there; return to where you were.

A. *Did you leave your umbrella at the restaurant we just left?*
B. *Yes, and I'm going back to get it.*

come back Return here; return to where you now are. *We like this city and we'll come back (here) next year.* (*Come back* can also be a form of polite goodbye as in *Come back any time. You're always welcome at our home.* It means only that the people who had invited you enjoyed your visit and may invite you again.)

Compare: **get back.**

from now on Starting this moment and continuing into the future—used only with present and future tenses.

A. *Does Mary tell the truth?*
B. *Yes, always.*
C. *Well, from now on I'm going to believe her.*

Compare: **from then on.**

see to Take steps to do or cause to happen; give attention to—followed by a noun or pronoun. The omitted verbal idea is often understood from the context. *It's noon. We must see to (making) lunch.*

Equivalent: **see about.**
Contrast: **not to bother with.**

What is the matter? Is there a trouble or difficulty? Is something wrong physically or mentally? *You look unhappy. What's the matter?*

Compare: **what's the matter with** + noun or pronoun. *What's the matter with Mary?* Depending on the situation and the speaker's tone of voice, the question may suggest that Mary is acting strangely or coldly.

SPELLING

go back • come back • from now on • see to • what's the matter?
Write or say the appropriate idiom. Use one letter for each blank.

Jane looked angry. "_/_/_/_'_ _/_/_ _/_/_/_/_/_?" her husband Jim asked her.

"I'm angry with myself. I left my umbrella at Society Bank."

"Take my advice," Jim said. "_/_/_/_ _/_/_ _/_ leave your umbrella and wear your raincoat instead."

"That's a good idea."

"Now _/_ _/_/_/_ to the bank and get your umbrella. Meantime I'll _/_/_

_/_ dinner," Jim told her. "I'll cook some hamburgers."

"You're a dear!"

"Of course I am. Dinner will be ready in twenty minutes. _/ / /_ _/ / /_ quickly."

SUBSTITUTING

Replace boldface words with appropriate idioms. Then copy or repeat aloud the whole sentence in the correct tense and person.

1. I failed my first math test, but **starting now** I'm going to study harder. ______________________________.
2. Our house needs painting. Will you **attend to it**? ______________________________.
3. Don't stay in Chicago. We miss you. **Return here**. ______________________________.
4. John left his hat at school, so he **returned there** for it. ______________________________.
5. **Was there something wrong**? At the party you looked sad. ______________________________?

CHOOSING

Write or say the appropriate idiom.

Last Tuesday I had a headache and stomach pains. "______________________________?" my boss asked. "Are you sick?"

He sent me to the company nurse. "She'll ____________________ you," he said. "She'll give you some medicine and send you home. ____________________ here when you feel better."

Of course, my mother was worried about me. "Stay in bed," she said, "And don't ____________________ to your job until you're well. And ____________________ you're going to eat a big breakfast. It will keep you well."

COMPLETING

go back • come back • from now on • what's the matter • see to
Give the appropriate idiom. Then finish the sentence in your own words, using the correct tense and person.

1. I can't start my car. I must get a mechanic to ________________ or ________________.
2. Ivan was homesick, so he left the United States and ________________ to ________________.
3. My teacher says that I don't study enough. ________________ I'm going to ________________.
4. We're waiting for you. When will you ________________ from ________________?
5. ________________ yesterday? Were you upset? You seemed ________________.

CONTEXTUALIZING

In your own words, write (or tell) a story. Include three idioms from this lesson and use the ideas below. (50 to 75 words)

1) Anne lives in Boston. 2) She often visits her relatives in Montreal. 3) She likes Canadian life. 4) She doesn't want to return to Boston. 5) Her mother wants her to return. 6) Anne's relatives help her to find a job in Montreal. 7) They phone her mother. 8) "There is nothing wrong," they say.

VALUING

Discuss (write about) the questions below, using your idioms.

Mimi is a native of France, a country well known for its culture and history. She considers France superior to other countries.

A. Do you feel the same way about your country? What are your reasons?
B. Americans talk a lot about their country. In your opinion, are they too proud? Do they talk as if other countries are inferior?

Colorful saying: Blow your own horn. Praise yourself by telling others how smart, skillful, or successful you are.

Lesson 2

IS SAM PREJUDICED?

ROLE PLAYING

Sam Trying to find someone?*

Mimi Yes, *you.** Tell me: Are you prejudiced against France?

Sam I'm not. How can I be? I know nothing about France . . . good or bad.

Mimi Everybody knows about France.

Sam I don't. What does your country look like? I don't know. What **goes on** there? I don't know. **What's more**, I know only one French person.

Mimi Someone you met in Japan?

Sam No, here in San Francisco. She **comes from** Paris and she's called Mimi. I like her.

Mimi I don't like you. You're against France.

Sam Listen a minute. Maybe you'll **change your mind.**

Mimi I'm listening.

Sam Every people is different. French, Japanese, Americans—they're all different. Not superior or inferior. Different. You ought to know this.

Mimi Are you calling *me* prejudiced?

Sam Maybe. But why not **get rid of** your prejudices? Then we can be friends.

Trying to find someone?* = **Are you *trying to find someone?*
Yes, you. = *Yes,* **I am trying to find** *you.*
For more information about sentences with missing words, see **Common Elliptical Constructions**, page 185.

IDIOM CHECK

go on Happen, occur. *What's going on? Why is everyone screaming?*

Synonym: **take place** Do not mistake this idiom for the **go on** which means "continue," as in *I won't go on working here. I dislike the boss.*

what's more Besides; in addition; moreover. *It's too late to leave now. What's more, it's beginning to rain hard.*

come from As an idiom, used only with simple tenses. Born or originates in; be a native to. *Twenty percent of American oil comes from Saudi Arabia./ The word* united *comes from Latin.* (That is, "united" was originally the Latin word "ūnus.")

Juan is Spanish; he comes from Spain.

Compare nonidiomatic use of *come*—move to where the speaker is. *My uncle Bill is coming from New York tonight.*

change (my, your, her, his, one's, our, their) **mind** Decide on a new plan; have a different purpose or opinion. *I changed my mind. I'm not marrying her.*

get rid of Free yourself of something unwanted or unneeded; discard as useless. *Get rid of that broken bed. We'll buy a new one./ Janet wants to get rid of her bad habits.*

Compare: **throw away** (used for things).

SPELLING

go on • what's more • come from • change mind • get rid of
Write or say the appropriate idiom. Use one letter for each blank.

My wife's parents are natives of Atlanta. She _/_/_/_/_ _/_/_/_ there, too. With a population of 541,467 people, it is the biggest city in Georgia. It is also the state capital. _/_/_/_'_ _/_/_/_, it's a center of business, education, and culture—something is always _/_/_/_/_ _/_ there.

Atlanta has only one disadvantage—like many large cities, it has too many robberies, holdups, and murders. But perhaps it will find a way to _/_/_ _/_/_ _/_ this problem. Then my wife and I might _/_/_/_/_/_ _/_/_ _/_/_/_/_ about living in Maine and return to Atlanta.

SUBSTITUTING

Replace boldface words with appropriate idioms. Then copy or repeat aloud the whole sentence in the correct tense and person.

1. Much of the world's coffee **is native to** Brazil. ______________________________

____.

2. Virginia **discards** her old clothes, but I keep mine. ______________________________

____.

3. Dr. Brown knows what **happens** when he leaves the classroom. ______________

____.

4. Your new coat costs too much. **Besides**, it doesn't look nice. ______________

____.

5. Marie and Anne won't go back to France this summer; they **decided differently**.

____.

CHOOSING

Write or say the appropriate idiom.

Ralph Fred always seems to know what's ____________________ in England. Does he ____________________ there?

Bess Yes, he's English.

Ralph Is he rich?

Bess I think so. He owns a Rolls Royce. ____________________, he has a chauffeur. But the man drives badly, so Fred wants to ____________________ the Rolls and fire his chauffeur.

Ralph The poor chauffeur!

Bess Don't worry. Fred will probably ____________________ and keep him.

COMPLETING

go on • what's more • come from • change mind • get rid of

Give the appropriate idiom. Then finish the sentence in your own words, using the correct tense and person.

1. Joan looks doubtful. Maybe she's going to ____________________ about_ _ _

_ _.

2. Camembert is a well-known cheese that ____________________ a country in

_ _.

3. France has many advantages. It has a good climate. ____________, it ____________________________________.

4. Marge needed more space in her bedroom, so she ____________ all ____________________________________.

5. Many strange things ____________ in San Francisco when ____________________________ two years ago.

CONTEXTUALIZING

In your own words, write (or tell) a story. Include three idioms from this lesson and use the ideas below. (50 to 75 words)

1) Ingrid is Swedish. 2) She wants to visit the United States. 3) Interesting things happen there. 4) One of her boyfriends is American. 5) He is rich. 6) "Marry me and come to the United States," he says to her. 7) Ingrid also has an Italian boyfriend. 8) He is very handsome. 9) Which boyfriend will she choose? 10) She cannot decide.

VALUING

Discuss (write about) the reactions below, using your idioms.

A. During a "break," a classmate asks your opinion of her country, which you dislike. How do you answer?

1. You walk away. It was a mistake to associate with her.
2. You say exactly what you think. (She can't be so stupid as not to know the truth already.)
3. You say what you feel but in the nicest way possible.
4. You say something about her country's having a "nice climate" and change the subject.
5. You make her happy by saying what you think she wants to hear. (As Zsa Zsa Gabor said, "How can you enjoy life if you always tell the truth?")

B. What would you say if someone openly criticized your country?

C. Can you be a friend of someone whose country is an enemy of yours?

Colorful saying: A pain in the neck. Said of somebody (something) who annoys you.

Lesson 3

MIMI INVITES SAM TO DINNER

ROLE PLAYING

Mimi I **ran into** Professor Smith yesterday.

Sam Where?

Mimi At *The Blind Samurai.* It's a good restaurant.

Sam It's too expensive for me. I cook my own meals and eat **at home.**

Mimi Are you a good cook?

Sam I open cans or heat TV dinners.*

Mimi Poor man! Come to my apartment Saturday night. I'll cook real food for you.

Sam To your apartment! At night!

Mimi Sam, you're in America now. You **have to** forget your Japanese ideas. Here a woman can invite a man to her apartment. It's not wrong.

Sam Excuse me. I wasn't thinking. I accept your invitation.

Mimi Now listen carefully: You will be coming from Shaker Heights, so **get on** the 41A bus. **Get off** at 33rd and Euclid. I live one block north, at 5 Maple Road.

*TV dinner = a ready-to-serve meal frozen in an aluminum tray. You heat the meal in an oven before you eat it.

IDIOM CHECK

run into Meet accidentally or unexpectedly. *What a surprise to* **run into** *Bob in the middle of New York City!*

Associated meaning: hit or collide with. *John was driving too fast and* **ran into** *a cop. He then* **ran into** *a brick wall.*

at home In your own house or apartment; the place where you live, often with your family. *I stay* **at home** *on rainy evenings.*

Compare: **at work, at play, at school, at church.**
Contrast: **at** *the* **home, at** *the* **play, at** *the* **school.**

have to + base form of verb. 1. Affirmative meaning: must—a command or a necessity. *The newspaper said he was dead, so it* **has to be** *true./ It's late. You* **have to leave.**

2. Negative meaning: are not obliged to—often excuses someone. *You* **don't have to stay** *at our party. We know that you're feeling ill.*

Contrast: **must not**

3. Polite meaning: It would please me if you do what I suggest—not a command. *You* **have to try** *my apple pie. I baked it especially for you.*

get on Climb on, step on, enter a bus, plane, train, boat, bicycle, horse. *George* **got on** *the plane at Chicago.*

Compare: **get in** (a car).

get off Climb off, step off, leave a bus, plane, train, boat, bicycle, horse. *At which bus stop do you* **get off**?

Compare: **get out** (of a car).

SPELLING

run into • at home • have to • get on • get off
Write or say the appropriate idiom. Use one letter for each blank.

Mimi's neighbors like to stay _/_ _/_/_/_ and play loud music until midnight. On weekends the noise doesn't bother her; she can sleep late. But on weekdays she _/_/_ _/_ get up at 7:00. At 8:10 she _/_/_/_ _/_ the Noble Road bus and rides to school. She often _/_/_/_ _/_/_/_ her noisy neighbors on the bus, but she doesn't even say hello to them. Ten minutes later they _/_/_ _/_/_ at the same stop as she does.

SUBSTITUTING

Replace boldface words with appropriate idioms. Then copy or repeat aloud the whole sentence in the correct tense and person.

1. Mimi **entered** the plane in Philadelphia. ____________________
____________________.

2. Sometimes Sam **accidentally meets** Mimi at a party. ____________________
____________________.

3. Mary's not **in her house**. She's at school. ____________________
____________________.

4. Sam **must** go to the doctor. He's very sick. ____________________
____________________.

5. Helga **left** the boat at New York. ____________________
____________________.

CHOOSING

Write or say the appropriate idiom.

In the past George ____________________ go to work every day. He __________ __________ the subway at Forest Hills, sat down for forty minutes, and __________ __________ at Fifth Avenue.

On the subway he met the same girl almost every day, so he started to say hello each time he ____________________ her.

Yesterday they became husband and wife. But she will continue to go to work and he will stay ____________________. He wants to be a house-husband.

COMPLETING

run into • at home • have to • get on • get off
Give the appropriate idiom. Then finish the sentence in your own words, using the correct tense and person.

1. The flight from New York to London lasted six hours. I__________________ my plane at London and_ _ _ _ _ _ _ _ _ _ _ _ _ _ _ _ _ _ _ _.
2. Mimi__________________ study hard now because_ _.
3. American bus drivers often carry no coins or bills. Before you__________________ a bus, you must be sure_ _ _ _ _ _ _ _ _ _ _ _ _ _ _ _ _ _ _ _.
4. Do you want to stay__________________ or_ _?
5. It was a wonderful party. I__________________ all kinds of_ _.

CONTEXTUALIZING

In your own words, write (or tell) a story. Include three idioms from this lesson and use the ideas below. (50 to 75 words)

1) Nancy is married to Bill. 2) He always wants to go to parties. 3) She likes to stay in her house. 4) But sometimes she steps on a plane and goes to New York. 5) He always takes the train to the West Coast. 6) Nancy and Bill have a perfect marriage. 7) They meet only accidentally.

____

____

____

____

____

____

____

____

____

____

____

____

____

____

____

VALUING

Discuss (write about) the situation below, using your idioms.

A. Mimi doesn't know Sam very well, but she will be alone with him in her apartment Saturday evening. Should she be alone in such a situation? What do you think?

1. Strongly against.
2. Against.
3. Not something you think about.
4. In favor.
5. Strongly in favor.

B. In your country, what circumstances (if any) allow a young unmarried man and woman to be alone together?

C. What do you think of young unmarried women who live apart from their parents? Who even live alone in their own apartments?

Colorful saying: Junk food. Manufactured food (often eaten for a snack) which contains little nourishment. Examples: Potato chips, soft drinks, candy bars.

Idiom Review of Lessons 1, 2, 3

Directions

a. Add letters to each circle so as to make an idiom.

b. Find the definition below that fits each idiom and put its *number* in the small circle.

c. Add the numbers in the circles across (⟶) or down (↓). The numbers *must* total 34. To help you start, four circles are already done.

Definitions

1. starting at this time and continuing
2. return there
3. decide differently
4. go into, enter (a bus, train, plane, boat)
5. meet by chance
6. have as a birthplace, place of origin
7. return here
8. Is there something wrong?
9. must; need to
10. besides; in addition
11. happen, occur
12. free yourself from something unwanted
13. give attention to
14. leave (a bus, train, plane, boat)
15. naturally
16. in your house

DO IT AGAIN, MIMI

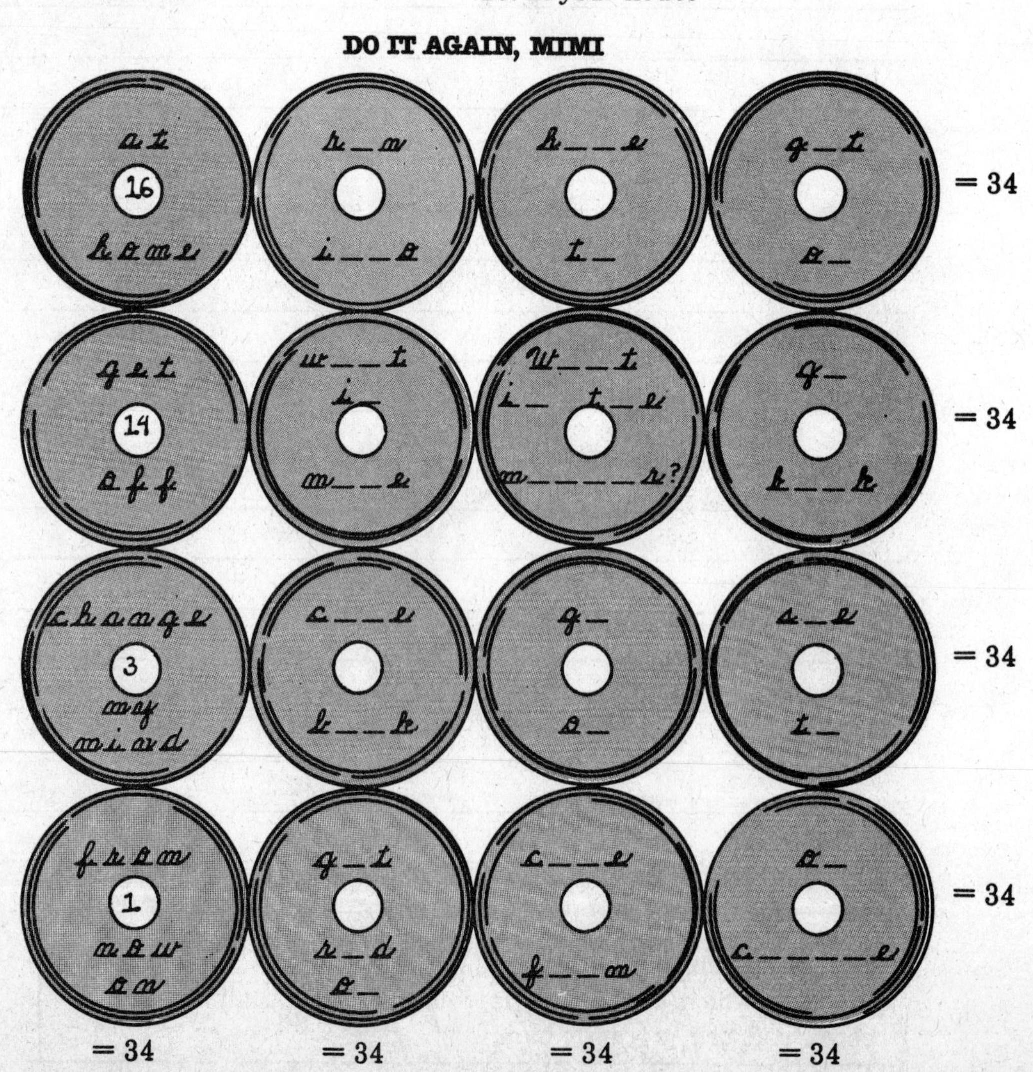

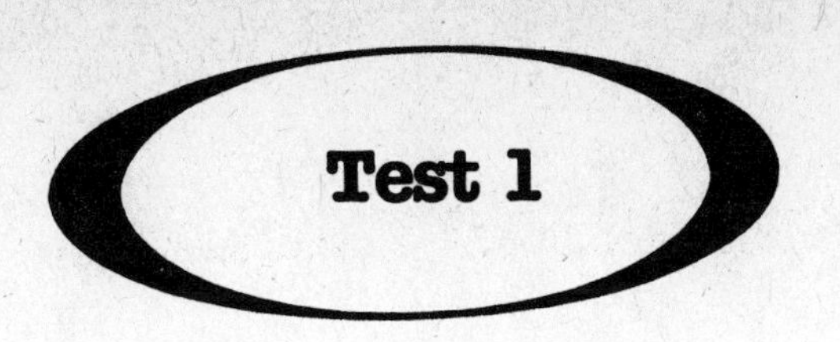

Test 1

Level I. From the **Completing** exercise of lessons 1, 2, 3, your teacher will choose five incomplete sentences and read them to you. Write them down, supply appropriate idioms for them, and finish them in your own words.

1 ______________________________

2 ______________________________

3 ______________________________

4 ______________________________

5 ______________________________

Level II. The pictures tell a story. In one paragraph of 60 to 90 words, tell this story or write it on a separate piece of paper. Include any four of these idioms: **what's the matter / go back / from now on / change (one's) mind / what's more / go on / run into / have to / get on / get off**

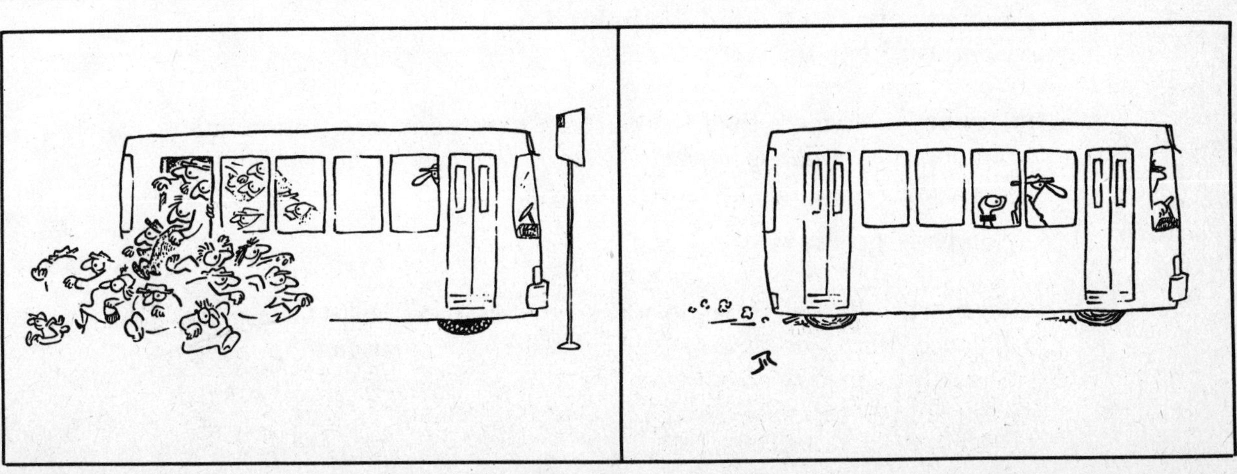

Lesson 4

WORK! WORK! WORK!

ROLE PLAYING

Sam I try to pay my electricity and gas bills within ten days or two weeks. But I always **get behind** on them.

Mimi Me, too. This month **I'm broke**. I don't even have enough money to **take a trip** to Cleveland. My aunt lives there.

Sam Why don't you go by bus? Bus travel is cheap.

Mimi That's true. But what can you do on a bus except sleep?

Sam Well, I look at the scenery and **at the same time** I do my homework.

Mimi Don't you ever take **time off** and relax?

Sam I feel uncomfortable when I'm not working. I live to work. It's because I'm Japanese.

Mimi Not me. I work to live. It's because I'm French.

IDIOM CHECK

get behind + *with, on, in* Do something too slowly; fail in performing an act. *Don't get behind in (on, with) your homework. You must pass it in next Friday at the latest./ Bob got behind on (in, with) his rent payments and had to leave his apartment.*

Equivalents: **fall behind, be behind.**
Contrast: **keep up.**

be broke Owe more than you can pay; have no money—often only temporarily. *Anita is broke; she spent all her money on clothes yesterday.* (Anita has no money today.)

Compare: **go broke.**

take a trip Travel to some place; go for a journey *of a certain distance. Mary took a trip to Chicago to see her mother. In the past she had only to go to the next street.*

at the same time Happening in the same moment or period of time. *My wife can laugh and cry at the same time.*

time off A period of release from work; time for yourself. *My boss gave me time off to go to the dentist.*

Compare: **time out.**

SPELLING

get behind • be broke • take a trip • at the same time • time off
Write or say the appropriate idiom. Use one letter for each blank.

How can my son watch TV and do his homework _/_ _/_/_ _/_/_/_ _/_/_/_? How can he _/_/_ _/_/_/_/_/_ in all his courses and still receive A's? How can he have $20 one day, _/_ _/_/_/_/_ the next, but not buy anything? How can he _/_/_/_ __ _/_/_/_ to Hawaii, spend two weeks there, but still like the climate in New York better?

Maybe I'll take _/_/_/_ _/_/_ from being a father and try being a teenager for a few days. I need some answers.

SUBSTITUTING

Replace boldface words with appropriate idioms. Then copy or repeat aloud the whole sentence in the correct tense and person.

1. Oliver **travels** to Spain every summer. ______________________________
______________________________.
2. The post office **was late** in delivering the Christmas mail. ______________________________
______________________________.
3. We all need **a period of release from work** to relax. ______________________________
______________________________.
4. My brother **has no money**; he can't even pay his rent. ______________________________
______________________________.
5. The two horses crossed the finish line **together**. ______________________________
______________________________.

CHOOSING

Write or say the appropriate idiom.

Last week Lily had some ______________________, so she ____________________ to Paris. During the whole week she ate only at three-star restaurants. ____________ ___________ she bought seven dresses, four sweaters, four skirts, and three pairs of shoes.

She flew home on Sunday. On Monday she had to borrow money for her rent and her phone bill. She ______________________, of course, but she didn't want to ________ ______________ in her payments.

COMPLETING

get behind • be broke • take a trip • at the same time • time off

Give the appropriate idiom. Then finish the sentence in your own words, using the correct tense and person.

1. (Where are you going on vacation this summer?) I ____________________ to _ .
2. Jerry spent all his money on clothes. He ____________________ now, so he _ .
3. My girlfriend could do two things____________________. She could_ .
4. Sam works too hard. He needs to take ____________________ and relax, or he _ .
5. Don't____________________ in your homework because_ .

CONTEXTUALIZING

In your own words, write (or tell) a story. Include three idioms from this lesson and use the ideas below. (50 to 75 words)

1) Sam had a dream. 2) Bread cost $1 a loaf. 3) Milk cost $1.20 a quart. 4) His room cost $300 a month. 5) He worked without stopping. 6) But he never had any money. 7) He wasn't able to pay his bills. 8) He wasn't able to go home. 9) His alarm clock rang and he opened his eyes. 10) "How terrible!" he said. "My dream isn't a dream."

VALUING

Discuss (write about) your ratings, using your idioms.

A. A person may be: 1) kind, 2) intelligent, 3) physically attractive, 4) hard working, 5) honest, 6) faithful, 7) brave.

In what order would you rank these qualities in a husband? In a wife? In a friend? Why?

B. Many Americans work hard. They believe that work is good for people. For some of them, work is the most important thing in life. How do you feel about this attitude?

C. Do you, personally, work to live? Live to work?

Colorful saying: Knock yourself out. Work very hard; make a tremendous effort to do something.

Lesson 5

ARE AMERICANS IMPOLITE?

ROLE PLAYING

Mimi **On the whole**, Americans aren't polite. Most of them have bad manners.

Sam Really!

Mimi Well, what do you **think of** strangers who call you by your first name? On Wednesday I moved into my apartment. On Thursday the janitor came to fix the heating. **Right away** he called me Anne-Marie. The next day the postman called me Annie. **In fact**, two minutes after they meet me, Americans begin inventing names for me.

Sam But it's an American custom. They only mean to be friendly.

Mimi We **are used to** politeness in France.

Sam But customs are different in your country. That's why some American tourists **think of** the French as unfriendly.

Mimi They're idiots!

IDIOM CHECK

on the whole With few exceptions; in general. *On the whole, men are taller than women.*

Equivalent: **by and large.**

think of —not used in continuous tenses. Have an opinion on something; consider it good or bad. *What does Mimi think of Sam? She thinks of him as honest and intelligent.*

Compare: **think of**, meaning *reflect upon: Are you thinking of your old age and saving your money?*

right away Immediately; without delay. *Please answer the phone right away.*

Synonym: **right off.**
Contrast: **after a while.**

in fact Really; in reality. *Hitler isn't dead. In fact, he's alive and living in Paraguay./ Mimi didn't believe Sam. In fact, she called him a liar.* (Often used for emphasis: She *even* called him a liar.)

Equivalent: **in point of fact.**

be used to + *ing* Be accustomed to; have the habit of. *John is used to smoking cigars./ For many years Henry walked in his sleep. His wife was used to it.*

Contrast: **used to** (lesson 13).

SPELLING

on the whole • think of • right away • in fact • be used to
Write or say the appropriate idiom. Use one letter for each blank.

Dick _/_ _/ / /_ _/_ smoking big, black, smelly cigars in buses. _/_ _/ /_ _/ / / /_, the passengers dislike his cigars and they _/ / / /_ _/_ him as impolite. But he doesn't care. _/_ _/ / /_, he never stops smoking. He finishes one cigar and starts another _/ / / /_ _/ / /_.

SUBSTITUTING

Replace boldface words with appropriate idioms. Then copy or repeat aloud the whole sentence in the correct tense and person.

1. My brother has a temperature of 103°. I'm phoning a doctor **immediately.** ____.
2. Frank likes Helena very much; **really**, he loves her. ____.
3. I **have the habit of** sleeping late on weekends ____.
4. **In general**, children start talking around age 2. ____.
5. What **opinion** do you **have on** birth control? ____.

CHOOSING

Write or say the appropriate idiom.

Mimi's American friends were accustomed to eating frozen fish, canned vegetables, and soup in packages. ____________________, some of them *never* ate fresh food! But Mimi ____________________ eating fresh fruit and vegetables and fish. When she tasted something fresh, she knew it ____________________.

What was Mimi's opinion of American food? She ____________________ most of it as tasteless and, ____________________, she disliked it.

COMPLETING

on the whole • think of • right away • in fact • be used to
Give the appropriate idiom. Then finish the sentence in your own words, using the correct tense and person.

1. The taxi came ____________________ because _ .
2. It is difficult to talk about American women in general. ____________________, however, they are _ _ _ _ _ _ _ _ _ _ _ _ _ _ _ _ _ _ _ .
3. Mimi respected Sam, but he ____________________ her as _ .
4. I think so. ____________________, I'm almost certain that _ .
5. In the past, we ____________________ drinking wine whenever there was _ .

CONTEXTUALIZING

In your own words, write (or tell) a story. Include three idioms from this lesson and use the ideas below. (50 to 75 words)

1) Sam has a habit: He always drives Japanese cars. 2) He likes them very much. 3) Almost all Japanese people like them. 4) These cars are well made and look nice. 5) Today Sam received a big check from home. 6) He is buying a Japanese car as quickly as he can.

VALUING

Discuss (write about) your choice, using your idioms.

A. Your ESL teacher is a 35-year-old woman, Mrs. Jane Smith. She asks you to call her Jane. How do you feel about her request?

1. You feel that she wants to be your friend and you use her first name freely.
2. You know that she wants you to relax, but you feel uneasy when you call her Jane.
3. You avoid calling her by name.
4. You continue to call her "Mrs. Smith."

Give reasons for your choice.

B. Are there persons who call you by your first name but whom you call by their last name? Why?

C. Some American parents allow (or ask) their children to call them by their first name. What do you think of this? Why do these parents allow this?

Colorful saying: Put your foot in your mouth. Say something foolish or impolite without thinking.

Lesson 6

WHAT TIME? FRENCH OR AMERICAN?

ROLE PLAYING

Sam Ready, Mimi? The Browns expect us at seven for dinner. We **had better** leave right away or we'll be late.

Mimi Why worry? People are always late for dinner.

Sam In France you can come late. Here you must come **on time**. When dinner is for seven, you come at seven, not eight.

Mimi Who told you?

Sam **Quite a few** Americans told me so. They **talked** it **over** with me and told me not to be late.

Mimi Okay, but first I have to fix my hair.

Sam Oh, no! We'll arrive just **in time** for dessert.

IDIOM CHECK

had better—unchanging modal followed by base form of verb. Would be to your advantage to do so; otherwise, something bad may happen. *It looks like rain; you had better WEAR your raincoat./ We had better LEAVE the party now or we'll miss the last bus.*

Very informal equivalent: **had best.**

on time Exactly at a fixed time; not late. *Dr. Smith always arrives on time. He enters his classroom at exactly 8:00 a.m.*

Contrast: **behind time, in time,** and **ahead of time.**

in time With sufficient time, early enough to do something. *I was late leaving home. But the bus was not on time, so I got to the stop in time to catch it./ We got to school in time to talk to our teacher before our class.*

quite a few (noun or adjective phrase) Many; a fairly large number. *It was snowing hard, but quite a few students went to school./ Yes, quite a few were there.*

Compare: **a number of.**
Contrast: **few** (*It was snowing hard, so few students went to school.*)

talk (something) **over** /S/* Discuss; try to agree or decide on by conversing. *Our family talked over our vacation plans and we decided to go to Hawaii.*

> */S/ means *Separable Idiom.* A separable idiom is a kind of two-word verb that you can separate into two parts. Between these two parts, you may or may not put the noun object (n.o.). But you *must* put the pronoun object there.
>
> a. We *talked* our problems (n.o.) *over.* Or: We *talked over* our problems (n.o.).
>
> b. We *talked* them (p.o.) *over.* (You have no choice: the pronoun must separate the idiom.)
>
> c. John *got on* the bus. He *got on* it at eight. (This idiom is NOT separable. A noun or pronoun cannot go between its words.

SPELLING

had better • on time • in time • quite a few • talk over
Write or say the appropriate idiom. Use one letter for each blank.

Dinner invitations in America are usually for any time between 6 and 8:00 p.m. If you are invited to dinner, listen carefully to what your hosts say about time. Are you invited to come *about seven* or *at seven*? *About seven* means that you may come as late as 7:20 and that you will still be _/_ _/_/_/_ to eat dinner with everybody else. However, for your first visit, you _/_/_ _/_/_/_/_/_ come _/_ _/_/_/_ —exactly at seven—but *not* ahead of time. (Your host may be in the shower!)

About seven may also mean that there will be cocktails (alcoholic drinks) before dinner. If you don't drink (or there are certain foods you don't eat), say so. _/_/_/_ it _/_/_/_ with your host or hostess. _/_/_/_/_ _ _/_/_ Americans don't drink (alcohol), so there is no problem: your host or hostess will see to it that you get a Coke or some fruit juice.

SUBSTITUTING

Replace boldface words with appropriate idioms. Then copy or repeat aloud the whole sentence in the correct tense and person.

1. You **ought to** wash your hands; they're dirty. ______________________________
   ______________________________.
2. My doctor's appointment is at two. I must arrive **punctually**. ______________________________
   ______________________________.
3. I arrived home **with enough time** to take a bath before ______________________________
   ______________________________.
4. **Many** of Betty's friends are mine. ______________________________
   ______________________________.
5. Where are we going next summer? I'll **discuss it** with my wife. ______________________________
   ______________________________.

CHOOSING

Write or say the appropriate idiom.

Mimi My exam on the English novel is next week. I ______________________ begin to study for it soon. I want to finish studying ______________________ to do something else before the exam.

Sam Oh, you have plenty of time to study.

Mimi No, I have ______________________ novels to read.

Sam How can I help?

Mimi Can you discuss them with me now?

Sam I can't ______________________ anything with you now. My ESL grammar class begins exactly at one o'clock, and I have to arrive ______________________.

COMPLETING

had better • on time • in time • quite a few • talk over

Give the appropriate idiom. Then finish the sentence in your own words, using the correct tense and person.

1. The train was supposed to leave at 3:00 p.m. It didn't leave ______________________
   because _.

2. ____________________ of these jazz records belong _ _ _ _ _ _ _ _ _

_ .

3. I arrived at the bus stop ____________________ to get on _ _ _ _ _ _ _

_ .

4. Yesterday I ____________________ my problems with my friends. Now I _ _ _

_ .

5. We ____________________ buy new tires for our car. The old ones are _ _ _

_ .

CONTEXTUALIZING

In your own words, write (or tell) a story. Include three idioms from this lesson and use the ideas below. (50 to 75 words)

1) Marie was late to school. 2) She was late to work. 3) She was late to meetings with her friends. 4) She lost her friends. 5) Her boss discussed her "problem" with her. 6) She didn't listen to him. 7) She lost her job. 8) One afternoon she took a lot of sleeping pills. 9) Mrs. Green, her landlady, came to her room. 10) Marie was late in paying her rent. 11) Mrs. Green discovered her before something bad happened. 12) Lucky Marie!

____

____

____

____

____

____

____

____

____

____

____

____

____

____

____

____

____

____

VALUING

Discuss (write about) the questions below, using your idioms.

A. In your country, how important is it that you arrive at a business meeting on time? 1) Very important? 2) Important? 3) Not very important? 4) Unimportant? Can you say why?

B. If you are invited to dinner in your country, must you be on time? If not, how late can you be without being impolite? What about in the United States?

C. What happens if you are late to class in your country? In the United States?

D. What kind of proverbs do your people have about time?

Colorful saying: Give someone a hard time. Cause great difficulty to someone. Refuse a person what he or she wants.

Idiom Review of Lessons 4, 5, 6

Directions

a. Add letters to each circle so as to make an idiom.

b. Find the definition below that fits each idiom and put its *number* in the small circle.

c. Add the numbers in the circles across (→) or down (↓). The numbers *must* total 34. To help you start, one circle is already done.

Definitions

1. a pause from work or duty
2. ought to, would be smart to
3. in truth, actually, really
4. early enough
5. many, a large number of
6. happening at the same moment
7. be without money
8. without delay
9. discuss
10. in the habit of
11. have an opinion
12. go for a journey, travel somewhere
13. in general
14. exactly at the agreed time
15. fall behind schedule
16. irritate, trouble the peace of mind of someone

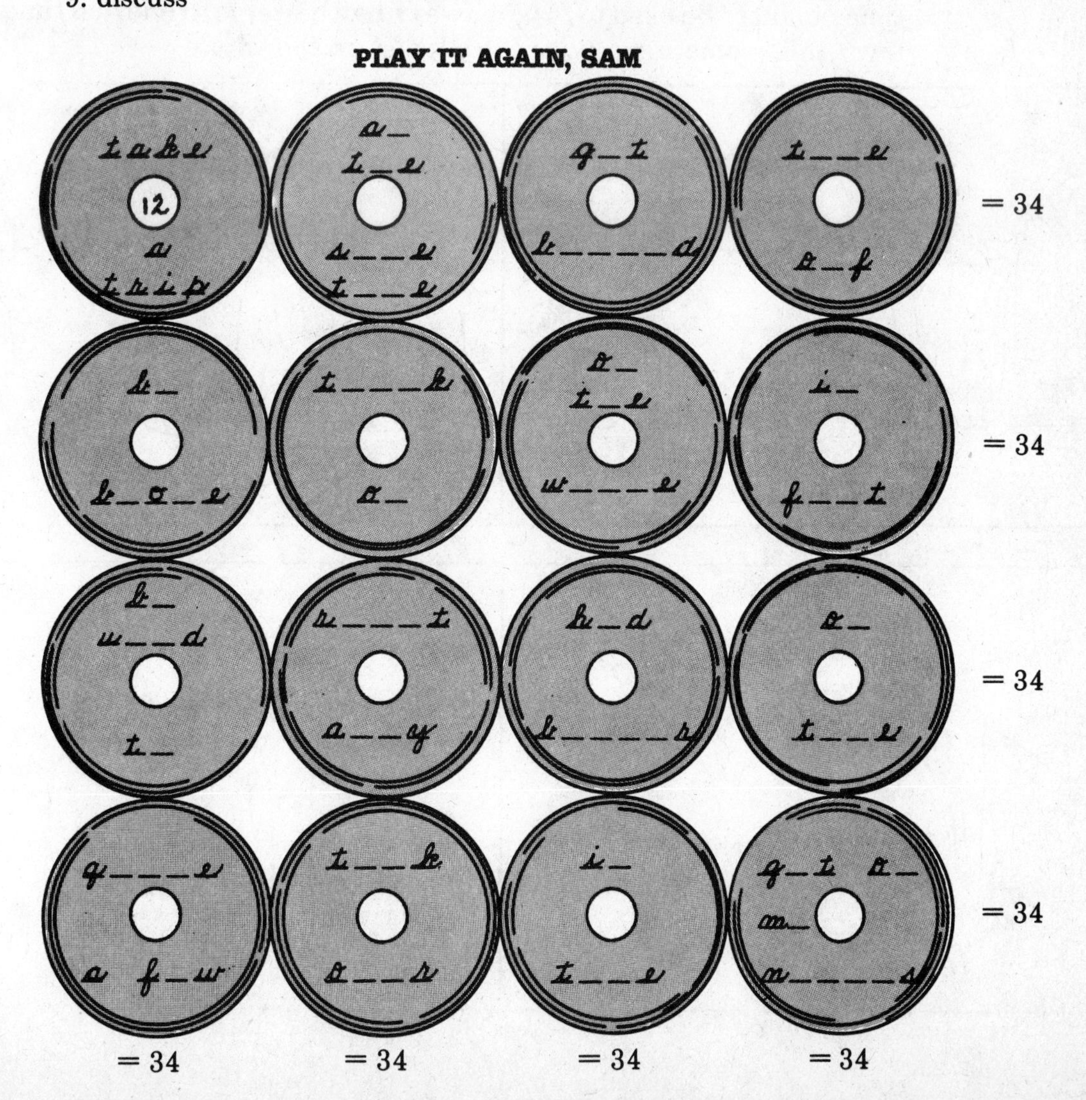

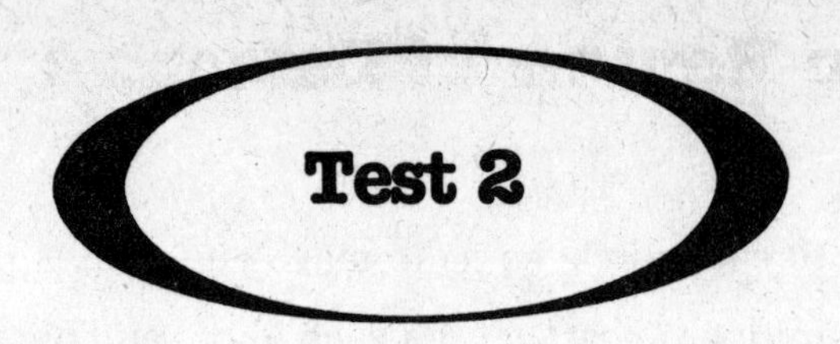

Test 2

Level I. From the **Completing** exercise of lessons 4, 5, 6, your teacher will choose five incomplete sentences and read them to you. Write them down, supply appropriate idioms for them, and finish them in your own words.

1 ______________________________

2 ______________________________

3 ______________________________

4 ______________________________

5 ______________________________

Level II. The pictures tell a story. In one paragraph of 60 to 90 words, tell this story or write it on a separate piece of paper. Include any four of these idioms: **at the same time / in fact / be used to / right away / had better / in time / on time / quite a few / talk (something) over / think of / on the whole**

Lesson 7

THE SCHOOL CAFETERIA: MIMI CRITICIZES AMERICAN BREAKFASTS

ROLE PLAYING

Sam Mimi, is that your breakfast—a cup of coffee?

Mimi French people don't like big breakfasts—**at (the) most** a cup of coffee and some bread.

Sam Lots of Americans eat a big breakfast—bacon, eggs, two or three pieces of toast, coffee. They eat some cereal, too.

Mimi **(It's) no wonder** that American TV always advertises medicine for sick stomachs or reducing pills for fat ones. Besides . . .

Sam Mimi, why do you choose . . . why do you **pick out** only bad things about Americans? Why do you **take advantage of** everything I say to criticize them?

Mimi Because I **have a good time** doing it. It's fun!

IDIOM CHECK

at (the) most No more than; as a maximum. *At (the) most he has $100 in the bank./ She left fifteen minutes ago at (the) most./ It was a small mistake at most.* (It wasn't much of a mistake.)

Contrast: **at the least.**

(it's) no wonder It's not surprising; it's to be expected. *Pat never did his homework; (it's) no wonder he failed the test.*

pick out /S/ a) Choose. *Pick out the movie you want to see.* b) Recognize from among surrounding persons or objects. *Bill has red hair. It's easy to pick him out in a crowd.*

take advantage of Profit from; use a particular opportunity to obtain something. *I took advantage of the weekend to see three movies./ Mimi knew Sam would do anything for her, so she took advantage of him.* (Mimi profited unfairly from Sam's feeling and made him do what she wanted.)

Synonym: **make the most of.**

have a good time Enjoy yourself; have fun. *Suzy always has a good time at parties.*

SPELLING

at (the) most • (it's) no wonder • pick out • take advantage of • have a good time
Write or say the appropriate idiom. Use one letter for each blank.

Carl earns only $95 a week. He spends __ ____ $30 a week on food. He has to ____ _________ __ sales at the supermarket and he ____ ___ old food that is selling at half price.

Rich people eat what they want, go where they want, do what they want. Their lives are fun; they're always ______ _ ____ ____.
__ ______ Carl wants to be rich.

SUBSTITUTING

Replace boldface words with appropriate idioms. Then copy or repeat aloud the whole sentence in the correct tense and person.

1. You're late. You have **no more than** ten minutes to get there. ____________________.
2. He's always eating candy; **it's not surprising** he's fat. ____________________.
3. Teddy **chose** a beautiful ring for his girlfriend. ____________________.
4. Doris is **profiting from** her weekends to play golf. ____________________.
5. I **enjoy myself** watching football on TV. ____________________.

CHOOSING

Write or say the appropriate idiom.

I don't like buying a new suit. It takes me such a long time to ______________ one ______________. Of course, I ____________________ my girlfriend's advice. But we have different tastes: She dislikes *almost* all my ties. ______________ she likes one or two. The same thing is true for the rest of my clothes. ____________________ we fight every time I buy a suit or coat. Believe me, a clothing store is no fun. I never ____________________ there.

COMPLETING

at (the) most • (it's) no wonder • pick out • take advantage of • have a good time
Give the appropriate idiom. Then finish the sentence in your own words, using the correct tense and person.

1. Jimmy likes to ski. He ____________________ his vacation next Christmas to _ .
2. You never save any money! ____________________ that you don't have _ .
3. My son's school is a half mile from our house ____________________. He can _ .
4. Will Mimi ____________________ at Sam's party? She seems _ .
5. Please buy me a good dictionary at the college bookstore. You can __________ one __________ and _ .

CONTEXTUALIZING

In your own words, write (or tell) a story. Include three idioms from this lesson and use the ideas below. (50 to 75 words)

1) Mary wanted to go to the seashore. 2) Her husband wanted to go to the mountains. 3) They had only two weeks vacation. 4) They chose the Rocky Mountains—for one week. 5) The second week they spent on the beach at San Diego. 6) They returned home happy. 7) They both had fun.

VALUING

Discuss (write about) your reactions, using your idioms.

A. Average Americans eat lots of canned food and frozen food. (Often chemicals—BHT and calcium propionate—are added so food stays "fresh" longer.) Americans often eat at "fast" food restaurants—McDonald's (50 billion hamburgers sold), for example. Try to compare everyday American food with your own. Does it: 1) Make you happy to eat it? 2) Surprise you but not unpleasantly? 3) Fill you and nourish you but nothing more? 4) Make you feel suspicious of all the chemicals in it? 5) Leave a bad taste in your mouth and a bad opinion of American people? Discuss your reasons.

B. Do you think that food can tell you something about national character? What does your country's food tell you about your country?

Colorful saying: Get your kicks (from). Obtain excitement, pleasure, or satisfaction from some particular thing or activity.

Lesson 8

WILL SAM WORK IN HIS UNDERWEAR?

ROLE PLAYING

Mimi The weather is getting hot. I'll have to **put on** a sweater.

Sam A sweater!

Mimi Because of my landlady's air conditioning. Two minutes after I get home, I start shivering. Then I **catch cold.**

Sam At my office we're supposed to keep the temperature at 65°. But all winter the temperature's at 72°. Everyone likes it that way. It's so warm that I feel like **taking off** my clothes and working in my underwear.

Mimi Maybe that's why so many Americans wear lightweight clothes in winter—to stay cool.

Sam Now that I **think** it **over**—yes, that has to be the reason. Maybe they ought to wear bathing suits in winter.

Mimi Sam, stop **finding fault with** Americans. Isn't that what *you* tell *me*?

Sam You're right! They may freeze us in summer and boil us in winter, but they're still nice people.

IDIOM CHECK

put on /S/ Dress in; clothe yourself or somebody else. *The mother put a dress on her baby./ Here's your hat. Put it on.*

catch (a) cold Become ill with a cold. *Dress warmly or you might catch cold.*

take off /S/ a) Remove—usually your clothes. *"Take your hat off," my father told me. "Always take it off in the house."* b) Leave the ground and rise—intransitive. *The plane took off.*

think (something) **over** /S/ Reflect upon; consider carefully before deciding.

a. **Saleswoman** Are you going to buy the skirt?
You *I'm not sure. I'll think it over.* (polite refusal)

b. **Salesman** Well, do you want the car for $7995?
You *I'll think over your offer and give you my answer tomorrow.* (possible acceptance)

c. **Your father** *Think over what I said, son.*
You *I'll think it over, Dad.* (Important advice or information: you must consider it carefully.)

find fault with Criticize something or someone; complain about; be dissatisfied with. *My boss always finds fault with my work.*

SPELLING

put on • catch (a) cold • take off • think over • find fault with
Write or say the appropriate idiom. Use one letter for each blank.

Last winter my wife and I _/ / / / / /_ _/ / / /_ several times from the freezing weather. We _/ / / / / / /_ it _/ / / /_ and decided to move to Hawaii. Now we never _/ / / /_ _/ / / / /_ _/ / / /_ the weather. If it becomes a little warm, we _/ / / /_ _/ / /_ our clothes and _/ / /_ _/ /_ our bathing suits.

SUBSTITUTING

Replace boldface words with appropriate idioms. Then copy or repeat aloud the whole sentence in the correct tense and person.

1. Tony **removed** his glasses every night. ________________________________

____.

2. Wear your overcoat today or you'll **become ill with a cold**. ______________

____.

3. George will **consider** the matter **carefully**; he can give his answer Friday. ________

____.

4. Before Sue cleans her house, she **dresses in** old clothes. ________________

____.

5. I do my best. Why do you always **criticize** me? ________________________

____?

CHOOSING

Write or say the appropriate idiom.

Tom went to a store to buy neckties. He took each tie, ____________ it ____________, and looked in a mirror. Then he ____________ it ____________ and tried another. Which tie did he want? Before he decided, he carefully ____________ it ____________.

But his wife criticized his neckties. She ____________ every one of them. Tom was secretly glad when she ____________ and had to stay in bed.

COMPLETING

put on • catch (a) cold • take off • think over • find fault with
Give the appropriate idiom. Then finish the sentence in your own words, using the correct tense and person.

1. Henry forgot to ____________ his raincoat and wear his rubbers each time _ .
2. ____________ what we studied in English this year and write an essay about _ .
3. My mother ____________ the way I dress. She dislikes _ .
4. Your clothes look dirty. Please ____________ and _ .
5. When I go to a wedding, I ____________ my best suit and _ .

CONTEXTUALIZING

In your own words, write (or tell) a story. Include three idioms from this lesson and use the ideas below. (50 to 75 words)

1) Jim wasn't feeling well at work Thursday. 2) He reflected and decided that whiskey was good for a cold. 3) He got his overcoat and went home. 4) Jim's wife came home at 6 p.m. 5) She found him in bed—drunk. 6) "I seem to have a cold," he said. 7) "You are still wearing your clothes," she said.

VALUING

Discuss (write about) your rating, using your idioms.

A. Each time fashions change, Georgette buys new clothes. George is just like her: He buys a new car every year. On a scale of 1 (you entirely approve: It's great to wear new clothes and drive a new car) to 5 (you entirely disapprove: Everything should be kept until no longer usable), *rate* George and Georgette. Then give your reasons.

B. In your country, what is the usual attitude toward waste? Does it depend on *what* is wasted?

C. With 6 percent of the world's population, the United States uses 30 percent of the world's energy. What should Americans do to save energy?

Colorful saying: Cool it! Calm down; relax; don't be excited or angry.

Lesson 9

IS GOD A WOMAN?

ROLE PLAYING

Mimi It's strange.

Sam What's strange?

Mimi That God's a man. People always say *He.* **How come?**

Sam No idea. It's a question I can't answer. I **give up.**

Mimi Not me. When I have a question I can't answer, I **bring** it **up** in class.

Sam **On the other hand**, lots of students don't **bring up** crazy questions in class. I would feel stupid doing it.

Mimi But Sam—God *could* be a woman. *He* could be *She.*

Sam But how will I ever **find out**?

Mimi *One day you will.* Until then, *you'd better* be nice to women.

IDIOM CHECK

give up /S/ Stop; renounce; abandon. *Give up smoking. You'll feel better afterwards./ Give him up; he isn't worth crying about.*

How come? Explain what you mean. How is it possible? *You're driving somebody else's car today. How come you're driving somebody else's car today?*

Compare: **What for?**
Equivalent: **Why?** (Note different word order: *Why ARE YOU driving somebody else's car today?*)

bring up /S/ Introduce a subject, idea, or question into a discussion. *It's a beautiful, warm day. Why don't you bring up the idea of a picnic with Sally?*

find out /S/ Learn or discover something new; get the facts. *What a surprise! I found out that Abdul is married./ Where does Dick live? Can you find out?*

on the other hand From the opposite point of view—conjunction used to contrast main clauses or sentetnces. *Mr. Carter may still want a typist. On the other hand, he may already have one./ Bill likes rock and roll. On the other hand, his girlfriend likes classical music.*

Compare: **on the one hand.**

SPELLING

give up • How come? • bring up • find out • on the other hand
Write or say the appropriate idiom. Use one letter for each blank.

Wine is both good and bad for people. I _/_/_/_/_ _/_/_ that it was bad for my stomach, so I had to _/_/_/_ it _/_. _/_ _/_/_ _/_/_/_/_ _/_/_/_, it was good for my nerves. In the past, whenever my wife _/_/_/_/_/_/_ _/_ the idea of buying something expensive, I always drank some more wine and said, smiling: "I'll think it over."

"Do you mean yes or no?" she'd ask. "_/_/_ _/_/_/_ you can't answer me?"

SUBSTITUTING

Replace boldface words with appropriate idioms. Then copy or repeat aloud the whole sentence in the correct tense and person.

1. I don't **mention** subjects that make my boss angry. ______________________
____.
2. I like visiting New York City. **From a different viewpoint**, I prefer living in New Orleans. ______________________
____.
3. Richard **stopped** riding horses after he broke his leg. ______________________
____.
4. I hope the detective **discovers** who stole my car. ______________________
____.
5. You didn't pass in your homework! **How was it possible?** ______________________
____.

CHOOSING

Write or say the appropriate idiom.

My son is lazy. If he doesn't discover the answer right away, he __________ trying. __________, my daughter never stops trying. First, she tries to __________ the answer at home. Next, she goes to the library. Finally, she __________ her question with friends. When they can't answer, they say: "Your questions are always hard. __________ you can't ask us something simple?"

COMPLETING

give up • How come? • bring up • find out • on the other hand

Give the appropriate idiom. Then finish the sentence in your own words, using the correct tense and person.

1. __________ you're late? Perhaps you can explain __________ .
2. When Jack __________ his mistake, he's going to __________ .
3. Ice cream was making her fat, so Janet __________ eating ice cream before __________ .
4. Her husband __________ the question of money each time she wanted __________ .
5. I like the way people live in Russia. __________, I don't like __________ .

CONTEXTUALIZING

In your own words, write (or tell) a story. Include three idioms from this lesson and use the ideas below. (50 to 75 words)

1) Perhaps smoking is bad for people. 2) Perhaps it is good for them—it keeps them thin. 3) When Peggy talked to her friends, she asked them about it. 4) The smokers pretended that they didn't hear the question. 5) Peggy finally learned about smoking from her doctor. 6) She decided to quit smoking.

VALUING

Discuss (write about) your viewpoint, using your idioms.

On October 8, 1983, Clifford Longley, religious affairs correspondent of the *Times* of London, summarized a pamphlet against "sexist language in the church" as follows: "*God* should never be *he* and Jesus should be *he* as little as possible. Even the devil should be sexless. . . ."

Feminists would be likely to agree with this pamphlet. As Ms. Jean Mayland (*Times*, October 13) says: "For many women the language of religion is increasingly hurtful and offensive in its use of *man* to describe us all."

Some of you ESL students are Christian and some of you are not. In *your* religion how do you feel about calling God *she* or both *he* and *she*? Do you think it's 1) a great idea, 2) certainly something worth considering, 3) an idea without importance, 4) a possible violation of your religion, 5) a criminal act against God?

Colorful saying: Out of this world. Extra good or satisfying.

Idiom Review of Lessons 7, 8, 9

Directions

a. Add letters to each circle so as to make an idiom.

b. Find the definition below that fits each idiom and put its *number* in the small circle.

c. Add the numbers in the circles across (⟶) or down (↓). The numbers *must* total 34. To help you start, one circle is already done.

Definitions

1. leave your bed
2. not more than; a maximum of
3. stop trying to accomplish or continue
4. enjoy yourself
5. use profitably
6. Can you explain?
7. remove; take from your own person
8. consider carefully and at length
9. it is not surprising
10. criticize
11. introduce a subject for discussion
12. learn, discover
13. become ill with a cold
14. wear; dress in
15. from the opposite point of view
16. select, choose

THEY'RE PLAYING OUR SONG

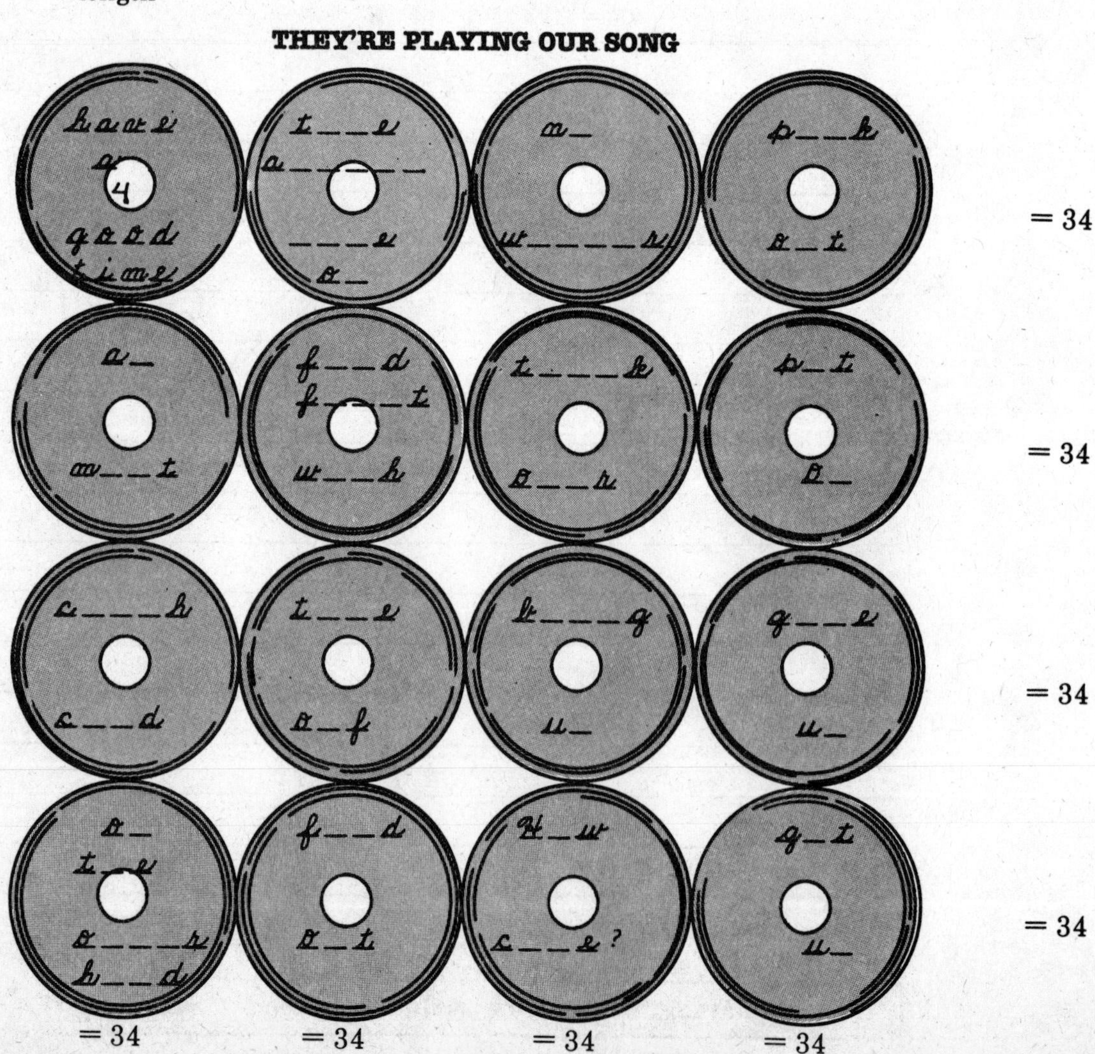

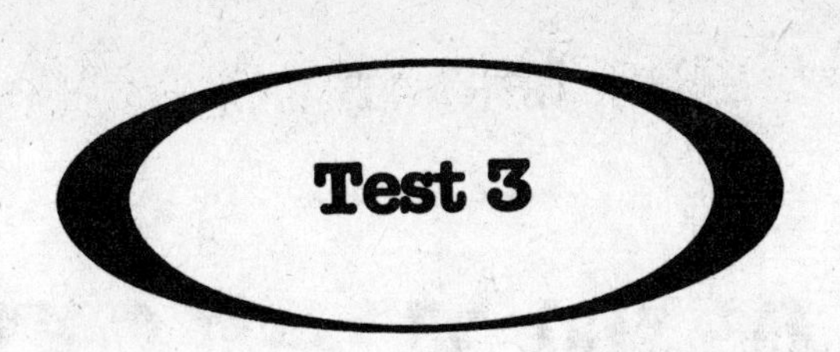

Test 3

Level I. From the **Completing** exercise of lessons 7, 8, 9, your teacher will choose five incomplete sentences and read them to you. Write them down, supply appropriate idioms for them, and finish them in your own words.

1 ______________________________

2 ______________________________

3 ______________________________

4 ______________________________

5 ______________________________

Level II. The pictures tell a story. In one paragraph of 70 to 100 words, tell this story or write it on a separate piece of paper. Include any five of these idioms: **at (the) most / pick out / (it's) no wonder / take advantage of / have a good time / catch cold / put on / think (something) over / find fault with / give up / find out**

Lesson 10

HEART ATTACKS: THE AMERICAN WAY OF DEATH

ROLE PLAYING

Mimi Why do so many American men have heart attacks?

Sam Because they're always **in a hurry**. They can't relax.

Mimi Or maybe men are the weaker sex.

Sam Well, my doctor says that too many men eat and smoke too much. But after forty, they don't exercise enough and they don't know how to relax. The result: heart attacks.

Mimi **What about** Sally's father?

Sam What *about* him?

Mimi He didn't smoke, ate like a bird, and played golf every weekend. So why did he have a heart attack? It doesn't **make sense.**

Sam **As for** him, he was very nervous and worked too hard. He **put in** sixty hours a week at his job.

Mimi Sam, I suddenly feel tired. **What about** taking me home early tonight?

IDIOM CHECK

in a hurry Needing to act quickly; rushed. *Ruth couldn't stop to talk. She was in a hurry to catch her train./ Bob really did his homework in a hurry: he made several mistakes.*

Synonym: **in a rush.**

make sense Can be understood; seems reasonable. *I knew so little English that my teacher's explanations didn't make sense./ It doesn't make sense to drive dangerously.*

as for Concerning; speaking of; referring to. *We have plenty of bread, and as for butter, I bought two pounds yesterday./ You can do what you want. As for me, I'm going to class.*

put in /S/ To spend time in a certain way. *Martha put in an hour a day learning to drive.*

What about? Would you like (doing something or going somewhere?)—often used in suggestions. *Husband: Is there something we can do tonight? Wife: What about (going to) a movie?*

Equivalent: **How about?**
Compare: **What about**, meaning: Concerning what subject? *Father: I want to talk to you. Boy: What about? I didn't do anything bad.*

SPELLING

in a hurry • make sense • as for • put in • what about
Write or say the appropriate idiom. Use one letter for each blank.

Bob Hard work makes me hungry. _/_/_/_ _/_/_/_/_ (eating) a hamburger?

Al Maybe hamburgers are okay for you, Bob. _/_ _/_/_ me, I hate them.

Bob Do you like hot dogs? We can eat them _/_ _ _/_/_/_/_, then relax a few minutes before our next job.

Al I don't like them either. But it _/_/_/_/_ _/_/_/_/_ to eat something. I'll take hot dogs.

Bob Good! It's decided. Now let's _/_/_ _/_ a few minutes eating and relaxing.

SUBSTITUTING

Replace boldface words with appropriate idioms. Then copy or repeat aloud the whole sentence in the correct tense and person.

1. **Would you like** going to a dance? ____________________
____?

2. It **seems reasonable** to save money. ____________________
____.

3. We **spent** six hours studying for our English test. ________________
____.

4. We're **rushed**; we're ten minutes late to the movie. ________________________
____.

5. **Speaking of** English, it's my best subject. ________________________
____.

CHOOSING

Write or say the appropriate idiom.

Sally was ____________________, so she decided to take a taxi. Taking a taxi was expensive, but it ____________________ to her: She wanted to get to the airport on time because she didn't feel like ____________________ three or four hours waiting for the next plane. She even said to her driver: " ____________________ going a little faster?" ____________________ him, he said yes but continued to drive at the same speed.

COMPLETING

in a hurry • make sense • as for • put in • what about

Give the appropriate idiom. Then finish the sentence in your own words, using the correct tense and person.

1. I can give you $5. ____________________ the rest, you'll _ _ _ _ _ _ _ _
_ .

2. Kids are always ____________________ to finish their meals and _ _ _ _ _
_ .

3. Marie ____________________ eight hours yesterday _ _ _ _ _ _ _ _
_ .

4. I don't want to go to the movies. ____________________ staying home and
_ ?

5. It doesn't ____________________ to work too hard. You might _ _ _ _ _ _
_ .

CONTEXTUALIZING

In your own words, write (or tell) a story. Include three idioms from this lesson and use the ideas below. (50 to 75 words)

1) Suzy has a boyfriend named Ahmed. 2) She is always impatient with him. 3) She always wants him to take her somewhere quickly. 4) Speaking of Ahmed, he thinks and acts differently from Suzy. 5) He spends ten hours a day driving a truck. 6) He is tired in the evening. 7) It doesn't seem reasonable to him to hurry here and there. 8) He wants to stay at home. 9) Suzy wants to go somewhere. 10) Could you suggest a solution for Suzy and Ahmed?

___

___

___

___

___

___

___

___

___

___

___

___

___

___

___

___

___

___

___

___

___

___

___

___

___

___

___

___

VALUING

Discuss (write about) your decision, using your idioms.

After six years at an American university, you graduate with honors. Now you and your friends have the opportunity to take a leisurely vacation together, all expenses paid. You are making last-minute arrangements; the plane is leaving in the morning. Suddenly you receive three telegrams and you must make some decisions:

1. FATHER ILL / STOP / DOCTORS CANNOT MAKE DIAGNOSIS / STOP / NEED YOUR SUPPORT / STOP / MOTHER /
   Sender's name and address: Shigero Shimoyama / 7-14-50 Chiyoda-ku, Tokyo, Japan
2. MUST GO TO EUROPE IN THREE DAYS TO STUDY / STOP / I LOVE YOU / STOP / NEED TO SPEND TIME WITH YOU / STOP / YOUR SWEETHEART / STOP /
   Sender's name and address: Yasuko Tamagawa / 1756 2nd Avenue, N.Y., N.Y.
3. MANAGER'S POSITION MUST BE FILLED IMMEDIATELY / STOP / YOUR QUALIFICATIONS EXCELLENT / STOP / SALARY $40,000 / INTERVIEW IN MEXICO CITY FRIDAY / STOP /
   Sender's name and address: Juan Rodriguez / 78 Calle Septima, Durango, Mexico

What do you decide? Why?

Colorful saying: Breaks your heart. Someone or something which causes you sorrow, disappointment, and grief.

Lesson 11

THE SEX-MAD AMERICANS

ROLE PLAYING

Mimi Sex! Sex! Sex! That's all Americans talk about!

Sam Aren't you making it seem worse than it is? Aren't you **going too far**?

Mimi I often eat dinner with Americans. They **have** me **over** and then we put in hours discussing sex.

Sam What about French people?

Mimi In France we know it exists, but we read and talk about other things.

Sam Do you? Some of your greatest authors—de Beauvoir, Sagan, Aymé—wrote about sex and their books are best sellers in France.

Mimi **All right**, I admit it. But what about American movies?

Sam Sometimes they **go too far**, I agree. But many French movies are **not at all** for children or sweet old ladies.

Mimi Sam, why do you attack the French each time I find fault with Americans?

Sam I was only joking.

Mimi I can **do without** your jokes.

IDIOM CHECK

go too far Pass beyond a certain limit; exceed what people consider right and proper. *Attending church in your underwear is going too far.*

have (someone) **over** /S/ Invite someone to your home. *We're having John over for lunch Friday.*

Equivalent: **have up (down)** Applies to someone living on a different floor of the same building.

all right Okay; satisfactory—indicates willingness or agreement. *Is it all right if we stay at home tonight?*

not at all Not in the least; not in the smallest degree. *It was summer, but the weather was not at all warm. It is not at all like her to be impolite.*

do without To live, study, or work without something; manage without it. *Our fridge is broken; we'll have to do without fresh meat until it's fixed.*

Equivalent: **go without.**
Compare: **get along, get by.**

SPELLING

go too far • have over • all right • not at all • do without
Write or say the appropriate idiom. Use one letter for each blank.

Once a week Mimi _/_/_ Sam _/_/_/_ and cooks a big meal for him. "Eat my lunch" she tells him, "and you won't be hungry for the rest of the day. You can even _/_ _/_/_/_/_/_/_ dinner." Then she asks him: "Is it _/_/_ _/_/_/_/_ if I serve you another French lunch next week?"

Sam is _/_/_ _/_ _/_/_ unhappy with Mimi's French cooking and he agrees right away. Is it _/_/_/_/_ _/_/_ _/_/_ to say that Sam's heart is in his stomach?

SUBSTITUTING

Replace boldface words with appropriate idioms. Then copy or repeat aloud the whole sentence in the correct tense and person.

1. Sam is **not very** sure that Mimi loves him. ______________________________
____.
2. It's **beyond what is right and proper** to take off your clothes in public. __________
____.
3. It's **okay** with me if we leave now. ______________________________
____.
4. Some people can **omit** sleep entirely. ______________________________
____.
5. Friday I'm **inviting** you for dinner. ______________________________
____.

CHOOSING

Write or say the appropriate idiom.

It is ________________ unusual for Americans to invite foreigners into their homes. They especially like to ________________ them ________________ for dinner. If you are a guest, phone ahead of time and ask if it's ________________ to dress informally. Usually you can wear what you want, but there are limits: It is ________________ to come in your underwear. Even Americans cannot ________________ some rules!

COMPLETING

go too far • have over • all right • not at all • do without
Give the appropriate idiom. Then finish the sentence in your own words, using the correct tense and person.

1. There's a party at Harry's tonight. Is it ________________ with you if _ ?
2. As a joke, John put ice down Marie's back. Don't you think it's ________________ when a man _ ?
3. Yesterday I ________________ some friends ________________ to my place and _ .
4. Josephine measured her waist. Then she ________________ lunch because she was _ .
5. We were ________________ unhappy that _ .

CONTEXTUALIZING

In your own words, write (or tell) a story. Include three idioms from this lesson and use the ideas below. (50 to 75 words)

1) Mrs. Brown bought a bikini. 2) Mr. Brown said, "It isn't right to wear so little clothing in public." 3) She told him: "Visit a beach and see what other women wear." 4) A friend of Mr. Brown's invited him to his seaside house. 5) On the beach he saw women in bikinis everywhere. 6) Now he doesn't know how much or how little women should wear.

VALUING

Discuss (write about) the story below, using your idioms.

Alligator River was full of man-eating alligators and it had no bridge across it. Abigail, who lived on one side of this river, wanted to reach her lover Gregory, who lived on the other side. She had no money, so she asked Sinbad, the boatman, to take her (as a favor) across the river. But Sinbad told her that if she had no money, she had to sleep with him as payment. She refused and went to her friend Ivan for help. But Ivan walked away, saying that her problems were no concern of his. In desperation, Abigail returned to Sinbad and agreed to his terms.

As soon as she got to the other side of the Alligator River, she threw herself into Gregory's arms. But when she admitted to Gregory that she had slept with Sinbad so that he would take her across the river, Gregory became angry, pushed her away, and would have nothing more to do with her. A few minutes later Abigail met her friend Slug. She told him what Gregory had done to her. Slug became very angry at Gregory and went looking for him. When Slug found Gregory, he began to beat him up. He beat up Gregory for hours and hours. As the sun set over the Alligator River, Abigail stood there, watching and laughing at what was happening to Gregory.

Directions: Rank each person in this story on a scale of one to five, one being the most evil and five being the least evil. Then say why you ranked them the way you did.

Colorful saying: X-rated. Movies, magazines, or literature judged as pornographic and not for children.

Lesson 12

FINDING A JOB

ROLE PLAYING

Mimi Is it difficult to **make a living** in the U.S.?

Sam Most people can. The average factory worker earns about $7.50 an hour.

Mimi And secretaries—how much do they earn?

Sam About $5.25 an hour. Why do you want to know?

Mimi A French friend **called on** me this morning. She came to tell me her troubles. She needs a job. **For the time being** she has only enough money to buy food. She can't pay her rent.

Sam She had better find a job soon.

Mimi She phoned employers **all day long** yesterday. But no one needed a secretary.

Sam She ought to read the want ads.* **Sooner or later** she'll find a job.

Mimi I hope so. Otherwise, she'll ask to stay with me.

*want ad—a notice in a newspaper saying that a job, a service, an employee is wanted.

IDIOM CHECK

make a living + *ING* Earn enough to keep alive. *Lena can't make a living (by) DoING part-time work. She needs a full-time job.*

Contrast: **live hand to mouth.**

call on Briefly visit someone (at his or her home or place of business). *Please call on me at my office and we'll talk over your proposition.*

Equivalent: **drop by.** Informal usage.

for the time being Temporarily; for a limited time. *We're living in Boston for the time being, but we're moving to Miami next year./ John didn't have a place to live, so he stayed with his uncle for the time being.*

Contrast: **for good; for a long time; for always.**

all day long For the whole day. *I had a headache all day long yesterday.*

Compare: **off and on.**

sooner or later At some unspecified time in the future; some day; eventually. *My brother is coming back home sooner or later./ Sooner or later Mary and Jim are going to get married. We are sure of it.*

SPELLING

make a living • call on • for the time being • all day long • sooner or later
Write or say the appropriate idiom. Use one letter for each blank.

As a translator, Jill now earns enough money to own a used car and to buy clothes. In other words, she can _/_/_/_ _ _/_/_/_/_/_, so _/_/_ _/_/_ _/_/_/_ _/_/_/_/_ she's satisfied with her job.

But _/_/_/_/_/_ _/_ _/_/_/_/_ she's going to want a better job. Then she will have to read the want ads and _/_/_/_ _/_ some businesspeople personally. Or she will stay home _/_/_ _/_/_ _/_/_/_ and phone for job interviews.

SUBSTITUTING

Replace boldface words with appropriate idioms. Then copy or repeat aloud the whole sentence in the correct tense and person.

1. Mildred wanted to eat later; **temporarily** she wasn't hungry. ____________________
____.

2. I'm going to be rich **some day**. ____________________
____.

3. Bess works **for the whole day**; in the evening she's tired. ____________________
____.

4. It's difficult to work only part-time and **earn enough to stay alive.** ____________________
____.

5. Between planes, we **briefly visited** our friends in Chicago. ____________________
____.

CHOOSING

Write or say the appropriate idiom.

For ten years Jim ________ by repairing TV sets. But then he and his wife Mary decided to buy a larger house. There were moving costs and expenses for new furniture, of course, but ________ they had enough money. However, a large house can be expensive and they knew that ________ they were going to need money for repairs.

Finally, Jim decided to borrow $10,000. He ________ quite a few bank managers and spent ________ going from one bank to another.

COMPLETING

make a living • call on • for the time being • all day long • sooner or later
Give the appropriate idiom. Then finish the sentence in your own words, using the correct tense and person.

1. All his life Mr. Brown ________ driving buses. Recently he decided to _.
2. It rained hard ________ Friday, but on Saturday _.
3. I have enough canned food ________, but by next Friday _.
4. Every day Virginia gets a little sicker. ________ she will _.
5. Will you ________ me at my office if _?

CONTEXTUALIZING

In your own words, write (or tell) a story. Include three idioms from this lesson and use the ideas below. (50 to 75 words)

1) Tom quit his job. 2) He enjoyed, temporarily, his free time. 3) He could relax for the whole day. 4) But he had no money for food, clothing, or rent. 5) "Oh well," he said, "I'll have to go back to work some day." 6) Then he had another idea: he began visiting a rich girlfriend. 7) Lucky Tom! He married her and never worked again.

VALUING

Discuss (write about) the Millers' decision, using your idioms.

The Miller family must make a major decision: move to a distant city or stay where they are. Both Mr. and Mrs. Miller work—one is a schoolteacher; the other is a chemist. The chemist was recently offered a fine job: research director for a company in another city. The job pays $45,000 a year with excellent chances of advancement.

BUT:
1. For a teacher, a good teaching job in a new city is hard to find.
2. The Miller children are happy at their present school.
3. The city where the Millers now live offers educational and cultural advantages.

YOU DECIDE: Should the Millers move? Give your reasons. (One more fact: *MRS.* MILLER IS THE CHEMIST.)

Question: Could a situation like that of the Millers happen in your country?

Colorful saying: Get the ax. Be fired; be cut off from a relationship or a job.

Idiom Review of Lessons 10, 11, 12

Directions

a. Add letters to each circle so as to make an idiom.

b. Find the definition below that fits each idiom and put its *number* in the small circle.

c. Add the numbers in the circles across (→) or down (↓). The numbers *must* total 34. To help you start, one circle is already done.

Definitions

1. early; before the time agreed on
2. temporarily; lasting only a limited time
3. concerning, referring to
4. invite to your home
5. to spend time in a particular way
6. the complete day
7. How would you like. . . ?
8. not in the least or smallest amount
9. exceed a limit considered right or proper
10. okay, satisfactory
11. needing to act quickly
12. visit someone's home or place of business
13. have a clear, reasonable meaning
14. sure to happen
15. earn enough to support life
16. live or manage without something

ENCORE!

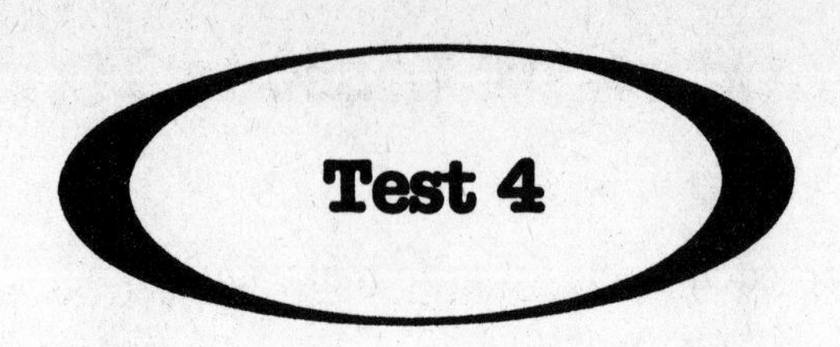

Test 4

Level I. From the **Completing** exercise of lessons 10, 11, 12, your teacher will choose five incomplete sentences and read them to you. Write them down, supply appropriate idioms for them, and finish them in your own words.

1 ____

2 ____

3 ____

4 ____

5 ____

Level II. The pictures tell a story. In one paragraph of 70 to 100 words, tell this story or write it on a separate piece of paper. Include any five of these idioms: **in a hurry / make sense / as for / put in / go too far / do without / all right / not at all / for the time being / sooner or later / all day long**

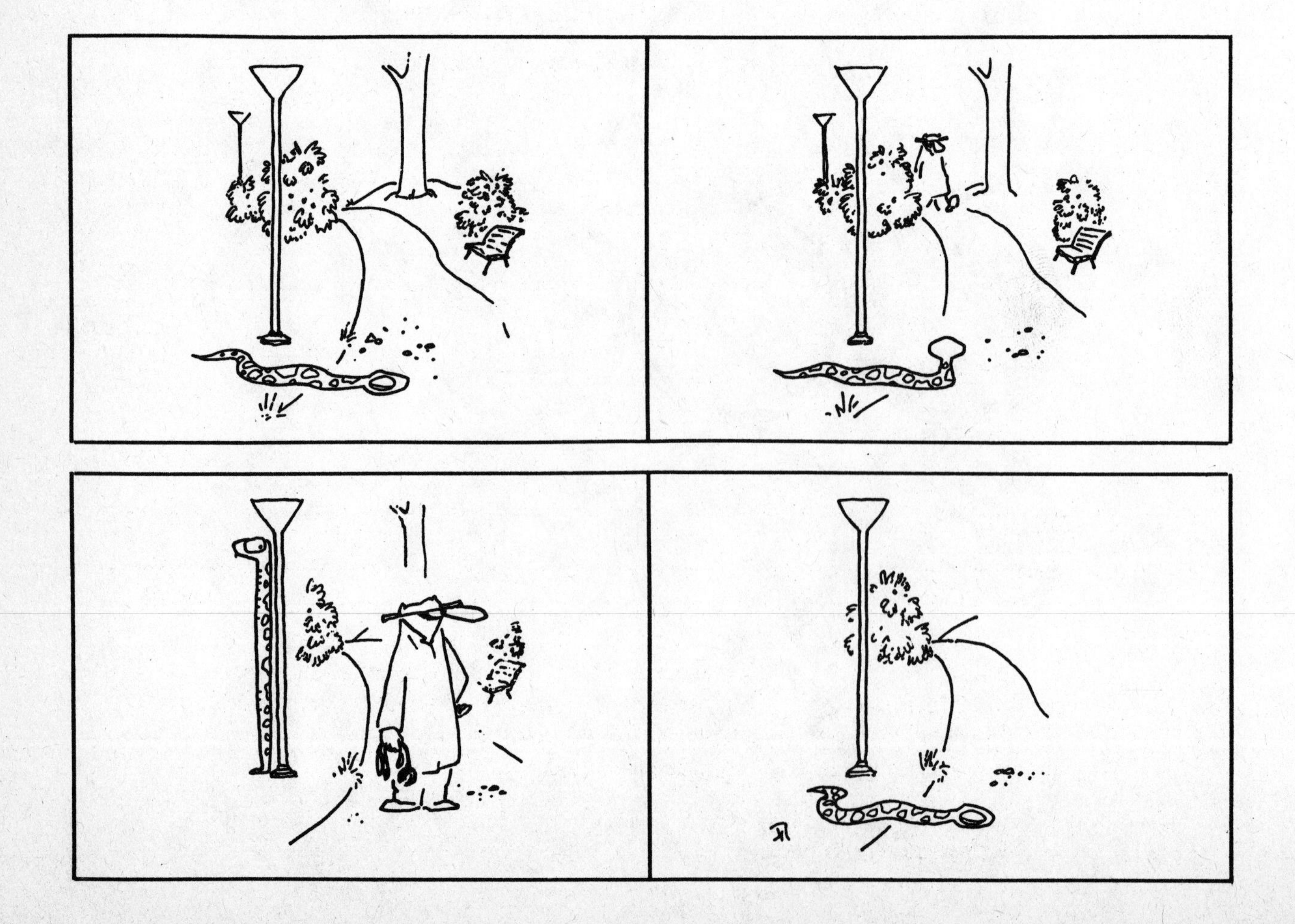

Lesson 13

ABOUT TIME

ROLE PLAYING

Mimi How can one word—*while*—mean minutes, hours, days, even years?

Sam You mean, like:
"Honey, when will you be back?"
"**In a while**, Frank."

Mimi And Frank's wife returns five hours later.

Sam *While* is a useful word. It's a balloon; it can become larger if she needs more time.

Mimi And **once in a while**? Is that a balloon, too?

Sam Yes, it can become as large as twenty years or more: Turkey has big earthquakes **once in a while**—which means every fifteen or twenty years.

Mimi So can you explain this *while*? Jane **used to** visit me **all the time**, but now she lives in another neighborhood and I see her only **once in a *while***.

Sam In the past Jane visited you almost every day—but now she visits, maybe, once or twice a month.

Mimi You're right!

Sam It's **about time** you admitted it.

IDIOM CHECK

in a while Later; at an unspecified time in the future. *Where's John? I don't know. I haven't seen him in a while.* (I haven't seen John for a number of minutes, days, weeks, or, according to the context, even months.) *Judy will be out to play in a while, but first she has to do her homework.* (Any time from a few minutes to two or three hours, depending on the amount of homework.)

Compare: **after a while.**
Contrast: **right away**

once in a while Occasionally; sometimes. *I eat pizza only once in a while because it's fattening./ Once in a while Bob would write his brother.*

all the time Continually; without stopping—may be used for emphasis. *Our factory stays open all the time, even on Sundays.*
FACTUAL STATEMENT: (Our factory stays open the whole week.)
EMPHASIS BY EXAGGERATION: *Joan talks all the time about how rich she is. I'm sick of it.*

Contrast: **once in a while.**

used to + base form of following verb Something that existed in the past; a repeated action or occurrence, a past habit. *John used to* **be** a salesman, but now he's a teacher. Mrs. Smith used to **smoke** fifty cigarettes a day.

Contrast: *I used to* **sleep** *until noon.* (I no longer do.) vs. *I am used to sleep***ing** *until noon.* (I still do.)

Lexical Note: *Used to* has two negative forms: *Used not to (use(d)n't to)* and the more informal *didn't use to.* Example: *John didn't use to* **smoke.**

about time Finally: said of something that should have occurred or been done earlier. *You've come! It's about time!* (Meaning: We were tired of waiting for you.)/ *It's about time that little Jimmy went to bed.* (Meaning: It's after the child's bedtime. He should already have been in bed.)

SPELLING

in a while • once in a while • all the time • used to • about time
Write or say the appropriate idiom. Use one letter for each blank.

My family _/_/_/_ _/_ enjoy sitting around our fireplace. My father would put in some wood and _/_ _ _/_/_/_/_ there was a big fire. In the past, we burned wood _/_/_ _/_/_ _/_/_/_. But now wood costs a lot and we have a fire only _/_/_/_ _/_ _ _/_/_/_/_. In fact, it's _/_/_/_/_ _/_/_/_ to admit it: We can't waste energy any more.

SUBSTITUTING

Replace boldface words with appropriate idioms. Then copy or repeat aloud the whole sentence in the correct tense and person.

1. I can't leave right away, but **later** I'll go with you. ______________________

____.

2. Ray gets all A's. Does he study **continually**? ______________________________ ?

3. I drove a taxi **in the past.** ______________________________ .

4. I **occasionally** phone my sister—on weekends mostly. ______________________________ .

5. Oliver finished his homework. **Finally**! His teacher was ready to fail him. ______________________________ .

CHOOSING

Write or say the appropriate idiom.

Juanita always ____________________ ask her father to play with her after dinner. She asked him ____________________ . He usually said, "It's ____________________ you went to bed." ____________________ , he said yes. Sometimes he would add: " ____________________ ." Then Juanita knew she had to wait a half hour or more.

COMPLETING

in a while • once in a while • all the time • used to • about time
Give the appropriate idiom. Then finish the sentence in your own words, using the correct tense and person.

1. Dave usually lies, but ____________________ he surprises us and _ .

2. My father ____________________ work as a policeman, but now _ .

3. I loved movies and I went to see them ____________________ . Now I am failing math because _ .

4. Henry wants to marry Sally. It's ____________________ that she _ .

5. I have no money to give you now, but ____________________ , maybe in three or four weeks, I can _ .

CONTEXTUALIZING

In your own words, write (or tell) a story. Include three idioms from this lesson and use the ideas below. (50 to 75 words)

1) In the past Edward was poor. 2) Maybe once or twice a month he had enough money for a movie. 3) He was ready for a change. 4) He decided to become a tightrope walker. 5) Maybe in the future he will be rich. 6) Maybe he will be dead. 7) No man likes people always to feel sorry for him.

VALUING

Discuss (write about) your problem below, using your idioms.

Good luck: A distant uncle dies and leaves you $1,000,000 inheritance.
Bad luck: Your doctor gives you six months to live.
Problem: What to do with all your money in such a short time.
Solution: Class votes on which student best solved the problem.
Reward: Winner inherits one shiny, new, American penny.

Colorful saying: To kill time. Do something, even something useless or boring, to make time pass more quickly.

Lesson 14

AMERICAN TV: FOR KIDS AND IDIOTS?

ROLE PLAYING

Sam I **make a point of** watching American TV. I learn a lot from it.

Mimi Are you crazy? It's for kids and idiots.

Sam TV national news is very adult. I **turn** it **on** every night at 6:30. It gives me the facts. It tells me what's going on everywhere. It helps me (to) **keep up with** the world.

Mimi The news lasts thirty minutes. What are you watching the rest of the day? Great ideas?

Sam Well, once in a while there are excellent movies.

Mimi But can you **put up with** five minutes of advertising after each ten minutes of movie? As for me, I **turn off** the sound whenever there's an advertisement.

Sam That's un-American of you.

IDIOM CHECK

make a point of Regard as important or necessary; give importance to + ING. *Sam was very polite. He made a point of thankING Professor Smith for each correction.*

turn on /S/ Start by turning or moving a knob, handle, or switch; start the operation of. *It's dark in this room. Turn on the lights. Turn them on right away.*

Equivalent: **put on.**

keep up with Be aware of; stay informed of. *My girlfriend kept up with the latest fashions and changed the length of her dresses every year.*

Synonym: **keep track of.**

put up with Tolerate; accept patiently. *Our teacher refused to put up with late students. He marked them absent.*

turn off/S/ Stop by turning or moving a knob, handle, or switch; stop the operation of something. *You're wasting electricity. Turn off the lights. Turn them off right away.*

Equivalent: **shut off.**

SPELLING

make a point of • turn on • keep up with • put up with • turn off
Write or say the appropriate idiom. Use one letter for each blank.

Jack _/_/_/_/_ _/_ _/_/_/_ his daughter's work in high school: He _/_/_/_/_ _ _/_/_/_/_ _/_ talking with her teachers and he never _/_/_/_ _/_ _/_/_/_ her getting low grades. Of course, he asks her to finish her homework before she _/_/_/_/_ _/_ the TV. She _/_/_/_/_ it _/_/_ when he tells her to.

SUBSTITUTING

Replace boldface words with appropriate idioms. Then copy or repeat aloud the whole sentence in the correct tense and person.

1. My wife **stopped** the vacuum cleaner. ______________________
______________________.
2. She **regards** driving her son to and from school **as important**. ______________________
______________________.
3. Sam **starts** his tape recorder when Dr. Smith defines new words. ______________________
______________________.
4. Please tell your kids to leave: I can't **accept** their noise any longer. ______________________
______________________.
5. Our doctor tries to **be aware of** new medical discoveries. ______________________
______________________.

CHOOSING

Write or say the appropriate idiom.

As a used-car salesman, I was very successful. Why? Because I tried hard to be informed and to ____________ recent sales techniques. I also ____________ finding out from other salesmen how they sold their cars.

Unfortunately, these men weren't like radios. I couldn't ____________ them ____________ when I wanted to listen to them and ____________ them ____________ when I didn't, so I had to ____________ a lot of stupid talk for one or two good ideas.

COMPLETING

make a point of • turn on • keep up with • put up with • turn off

Give the appropriate idiom. Then finish the sentence in your own words, using the correct tense and person.

1. There was a leaking faucet in our kitchen, so my father ____________ all the water in the house and _ _ _ _ _ _ _ _ _ _ _ _ _ _ _ _ _.
2. Professor Smith doesn't ____________ students who eat in class because _.
3. It was cold in the house, so I ____________ the heat and _ _ _ _ _. _.
4. My husband always remembers my birthday. He ____________ sending _.
5. World news is important. To ____________ what's going on, I _ _ _. _.

CONTEXTUALIZING

In your own words, write or tell a story. Include three idioms from this lesson and use the ideas below. (50 to 75 words)

1) Bob's children loved TV. 2) They started watching it after school every day. 3) They especially liked two TV cartoons—*Batman* and *The Flintstones*. 4) Bob disliked TV. 5) He made his children stop watching it. 6) They watched it when he wasn't at home. 7) They always wanted to know what was going to happen next on *Batman*.

VALUING

Discuss (write about) television below, using your idioms.

A. How much TV would you (do you) watch? NONE, 1 to 5 hours a week, 5 to 10 hours, 10 to 20 hours, MORE THAN 20 hours a week? Excluding news programs, what do you get from TV that is good? Bad? Simply entertaining or relaxing? On a scale of 1 (excellent) to 5 (terrible), how do you rate the TV in the country where you are now living? Why?

B. Who should decide what appears on TV?

C. Who should pay the cost of the programs?

D. Describe to a foreigner what TV (or radio) in your native country is like: What are its good points, its bad points? Can you say what makes it different from TV in the United States?

Colorful saying: Boob tube (also: **idiot box**). Because of bad and/or stupid TV programs, Americans may refer to their TV set this way.

Lesson 15

WANT TO GET MARRIED? GO SKIING

ROLE PLAYING

Mimi I'm **looking forward to** a Christmas vacation in the Rocky Mountains.

Sam What'll you do there?

Mimi I'm going skiing **as usual**. I go skiing every year.

Sam I **heard from** a friend yesterday. There was no snow anywhere in the West.

Mimi I'm hoping for **at least** twelve inches of snow. It depends on the weather at Aspen.

Sam Aspen, Colorado?

Mimi That's right. Why do you ask?

Sam To **make sure** we're going to the same place. I mean, I'm skiing there this Christmas, too.

Mimi Wonderful! We can go skiing together.

IDIOM CHECK

look forward to Anticipate, usually with pleasure; expect + *ING*. *How wonderful to meet you! I look forward to seeING you again./ Thank you for your invitation. We look forward to comING.* (Formula of politeness; indicates warm acceptance of the invitation.) YOU MUST NOT SAY: *I look forward to my father's death next week.* (This would indicate pleasure at the thought of his death.)

Contrast: **look back on/to.**

as usual As one very often does; in the customary way—in present tense, required a continuous verb. *Where am I going? I'm going to the movies as usual./ What did my wife drink this morning? As usual, (she drank) two cups of coffee.*

Compare: **usually.** *John usually told the truth.* (But not always.) *As usual, Mary told the truth.* (We expected her to tell the truth and she did.)

hear from Receive a letter, phone call, news, etc., from somebody. *Did you hear from Laura recently? She promised to write.*

at (the) least Not less or fewer than; a minimum of; at the smallest guess. *We should drink at least six glasses of water a day./ Barry is at least six feet tall.*

Contrast: **at (the) most.**

make sure + *of* or *about* with following prepositional phrase or gerund; + *to* before base form of verb Be certain of something; check; investigate carefully. *Make sure OF (ABOUT) your facts before you speak./ Sam made sure to lock his car doors. Sam made sure THAT he locked his car doors.*

SPELLING

look forward to • as usual • hear from • at least • make sure
Write or say the appropriate idiom. Use one letter for each blank.

I looked carefully at the letter to _/_/_/_ _/_/_/_ that it was from Sam. It was wonderful to _/_/_/_ _/_/_/_ him again, and I _/_/_/_/_/_ _/_/_/_/_/_/_ _/_ reading his letter.

I read it slowly. It was full of news and _/_ _/_/_/_/_ ten pages long. _/_ _/_/_/_/_, he wrote about many interesting things.

SUBSTITUTING

Replace boldface words with appropriate idioms. Then copy or repeat aloud the whole sentence in the correct tense and person.

1. I **anticipate with pleasure** your calling on me. ____________________
____.

2. **As she almost always did,** Jill finished her homework quickly. __________
____.

3. **Check** that you have our house keys. ____________________
____.

4. Norman owns **a minimum of** ten houses. ______________________________
____.

5. What is Ray doing now? Do you **receive news from** him once in a while? __________
____?

CHOOSING

Write or say the appropriate idiom.

Fred phoned me yesterday. It was good to ________________ him. He told me he was working hard— ________________ ten hours a day, sometimes more, and that he always got up early. He ________________ Sunday to sleep late.

Yesterday Fred got up at 5 a.m. ________________. He ________________ to rewind his alarm clock right away. Then he remembered it was Sunday.

COMPLETING

look forward to • as usual • hear from • at least • make sure

Give the appropriate idiom. Then finish the sentence in your own words, using the correct tense and person.

1. Because I am careful, I ________________ that all the lights are _ _ _ _
_ _.

2. ________________, our teacher gave us lots of homework and _ _ _ _
_ _.

3. The party will be fun. We ________________ going tomorrow night and having _.

4. The sky was very cloudy. It was ________________ 99 percent certain that
_ _.

5. At Christmas we get cards and we ________________ our friends, so we are happy to _.

CONTEXTUALIZING

In your own words, write (or tell) a story. Include three idioms from this lesson and use the ideas below. (50 to 75 words)

1) The American grading system uses 100 points. 2) 100 points means perfect work. 3) A student must receive a maximum of 60 points to pass a test. 4) It is customary in America for teachers to give several tests each term. 5) A student should check that he or she receives a passing grade on each test. 6) Mimi failed three tests this term. 7) She is afraid to receive news of her final grade.

VALUING

Discuss (write about) how to get a mate below, using your idioms.

A. Mimi wants Sam to be her husband, so she cooks wonderful French food for him. She even travels across the United States to be near him. In short, she does everything she can to attract him. How do you feel about Mimi's actions? To help you measure your feelings, your teacher will draw a line. At one end will be the words DOES NOTHING. At the other end, DOES EVERYTHING. *Decide how much a woman should do to attract a man.* Make an X somewhere on the line to indicate how much. After everyone marks the line, discuss the results.

B. Where on the line do you think the average young American woman would make her X?

C. And where would a young man from your country make his X? How much would (should) *he* do to attract a woman?

Colorful saying: Make time. Make successful romantic advances toward someone.

Idiom Review of Lessons 13, 14, 15

Directions

a. Add letters to each circle so as to make an idiom.

b. Find the definition below that fits each idiom and put its *number* in the small circle.

c. Add the numbers in the circles across (→) or down (↓). The numbers *must* total 34. To help you start, one circle is already done.

Definitions

1. not less than; a minimum of
2. start the flowing of water, gas, oil, etc.
3. expected or customary
4. continually
5. occasionally, sometimes
6. anticipate with pleasure
7. stop the flowing of water, gas, oil, etc.
8. later
9. finally! (it should have been done earlier.)
10. insist upon; emphasize
11. tolerate
12. receive news from someone by phone or letter
13. be certain; check
14. stay informed of
15. in the beginning
16. in the habit of

ONCE MORE

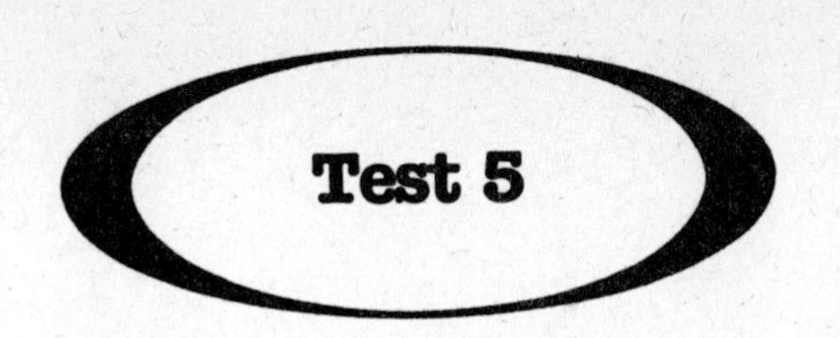

Test 5

Level I. From the **Completing** exercise of lessons 13, 14, 15, your teacher will choose five incomplete sentences and read them to you. Write them down, supply appropriate idioms for them, and finish them in your own words.

1 ______________________________

2 ______________________________

3 ______________________________

4 ______________________________

5 ______________________________

Level II. The pictures tell a story. In one paragraph of 80 to 120 words, tell this story or write it on a separate piece of paper. Include any five of these idioms: **once in a while / used to / all the time / about time / make a point of / put up with / as usual / make sure / look forward to / at least**

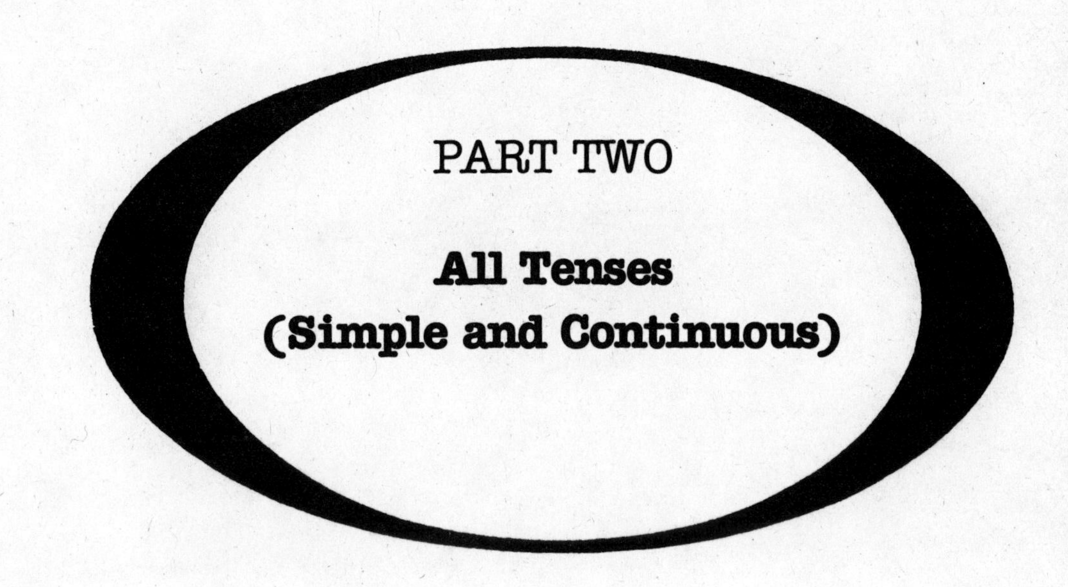

PART TWO

All Tenses (Simple and Continuous)

Lesson 16

AMERICAN LAST NAMES: A LESSON IN MULTIPLICATION

ROLE PLAYING

Mimi 3,000,000 Smiths! 2,500,000 Johnsons! Why are English names so common in America?

Sam Don't forget to include several million Americans named Williams, Brown, and Jones. Don't **leave** them **out**.

Mimi But what makes these names so popular? I can't **figure** it **out**.

Sam I couldn't **figure** it **out** either, so I **looked into** it. In 1790, Americans who came from England were **by far** the largest group here—69 percent of the population. Even then, Smith was a very popular name. Williams, Brown, and Jones were almost as popular—in both England and America.

Mimi So?

Sam So these English immigrants named Smith and Brown and Jones began multiplying earlier than—

Mimi Than nationalities that came later.

Sam That's right. And they **kept on** multiplying—at least eight times since 1790.

IDIOM CHECK

leave out /S/ Omit; fail to consider. *The printer left out two lines on this page./ Is the question too difficult? Then leave it out.*

Contrast: **put in.**

figure out /S/ Discover by reason; come to understand. *Sometimes Sam seemed to like Mimi; sometimes he didn't. No wonder that Mimi couldn't figure him out./ Can you figure out what Professor Smith wants us to do?*

look into Examine; investigate; study + ING. *David looked into buyING a new car and found out that he didn't have enough money./ Maybe Rita was murdered. The police are looking into it.*

by far Greatly; very much; by the largest margin. *Auto racing is fun, but it is by far the most dangerous sport I know./ Sam is the best student by far.*

keep on Continue; not stop + ING. *If you keep on tappING your pen, I'll go crazy./ Mimi kept on until she finished her homework.*

SPELLING

leave out • figure out • look into • by far • keep on
Write or say the appropriate idiom. Use one letter for each blank.

Tony Marco builds _/_ _/ /_ the most popular homes in San Francisco. He is so successful that he'll probably _/ / /_ _/_ building homes forever.

Is there a secret to his success? Yes. First, he considers each house individually and _/ / / /_ _/ / /_ the problems that must be solved. Second, he _/ / / / / /_ _/ /_ what people like and never _/ / / / /_ _/ /_ anything—even a nail—that might please them.

SUBSTITUTING

Replace boldface words with appropriate idioms. Then copy or repeat aloud the whole sentence in the correct tense and person.

1. My aunt is ninety, but she **continues** driving her car. ________________________
____.
2. Our manager will **investigate** the matter at once. ________________________
____.
3. Our boss doesn't speak clearly. Sometimes we can't **understand** what he's saying.
____.
4. Fischer is **very much** America's best chess player. ________________________
____.
5. John wrote the note so quickly that he **omitted** the "a" in *peace.* ____________
____.

CHOOSING

Write or say the appropriate idiom.

Because I was curious, I ____________ Don's past and found out that he was a thief. What's more, he stole more than other thieves: at least $10,000,000 a year. He was ____________ the greatest thief in the world. Another thing: he has ____________ stealing year after year. The police never caught him because he always thought carefully and ____________ how he could escape them. One day Don told me everything. He ____________ nothing—not the smallest detail—about his life of crime.

COMPLETING

leave out • figure out • look into • by far • keep on
Give the appropriate idiom. Then finish the sentence in your own words, using the correct tense and person.

1. For six months Sam ____________ telling Mimi that ____________________________.
2. Gilbert is examining the job market. He is ____________ jobs that ____________________________.
3. I have been ____________ the school's worst ____________________________.
4. We ____________ many capital letters from our writing until Professor Smith told us ____________________________.
5. Mimi hasn't understood whether or not Sam likes her. She hasn't ____________ what ____________________________.

CONTEXTUALIZING

In your own words, write (or tell) a story. Include three idioms from this lesson and use the ideas below. (60 to 85 words)

1) Ann Landers writes personal-help articles in American newspapers. 2) People with difficult personal problems send letters to her. 3) Unhappy husbands and lovers write her. 4) She answers all their letters. 5) She publishes only the most interesting ones. 6) She doesn't give the real names of people. 7) She tries to find an answer to their problems. 8) She examines all the possibilities. 9) She usually tells couples to stay married. 10) She is divorced herself.

VALUING

Discuss (write about) your viewpoint, using your idioms.

A. How do you feel about immigrants in your native country? How many people would you allow to come in? 1) None. It is hard enough for us to find jobs for our own citizens. 2) A small number of qualified people who can help our country. 3) A large number—anyone who is willing to work, even if he or she lacks technical and professional qualifications. 4) Anyone at all. (People from different countries, of different races, who practice different religions can add to our country's culture.) Other reasons for your choice?

B. The United States is rich and has plenty of land, so why shouldn't it accept anyone who wants to live here?

Colorful saying: Call (somebody) names. Use unkind or nasty words when talking to or about a person.

Lesson 17

A LAND OF IMMIGRANTS: SOME FACTS AND FIGURES

ROLE PLAYING

Mimi What about German-Americans and Irish-Americans? When did their ancestors come to America?

Sam Much later than the English did. Most of the Irish—**that is**, a million and a half of them—came between 1840 and 1855. In fact, many Irish-Americans live in the same cities as their immigrant great grandfathers. That's why Boston and New York phonebooks are full of O'Briens, Fitzgeralds, and Kennedys. As for German-Americans—

Mimi **By the way**, you forgot Chicago. There are thousands of Irish-Americans in Chicago, aren't there?

Sam Oh well, I can't remember everything. Now **let me see**... what was I saying?

Mimi German-Americans...

Sam Oh yes, German-Americans... Many of their ancestors came here after the 1848 revolution in Europe.

Mimi Can I **point out** that the names on American beer cans—Schlitz, Pabst, Schaeffer, Budweiser—are—

Sam German. I suppose you mean that making beer is one way of **taking part in** American life.

Mimi And *drinking* it is another.

IDIOM CHECK

that is To say it in another way; in other words—used to explain or give examples of a preceding idea, this connective usually has a semicolon (sometimes a dash) before it and a comma after it. *Debbie is a Californian; that is, she lives in California.*

by the way Incidentally; here's something to be added—an informal idiom which introduces something related to the subject of conversation or brought to mind by it. *First speaker: Mrs. Brown is well again; she looks marvelous. Second speaker: By the way, how is her husband? He's been looking tired lately.*

let . . . see Allow me/us to think about it—informal. *Let me see. How much time do I have before lunch?/ Let us see.* (More often: Let's see.) *Maybe we had better do our homework before we go to the movies.*

point out /S/ Explain; mention; direct someone's attention to. *Professor Smith pointed out Mimi's mistakes to her./ I'll point out some advantages of car insurance.*

take part in Participate, join, or share in. *John won't take part in football; he prefers acting with the drama club.*

SPELLING

that is • by the way • let . . . see • point out • take part in
Write or say the appropriate idiom. Use one letter for each blank.

Jack How would you like to ____ ____ __ a women's liberation meeting?

Bob ___ __ ___. Do you think I'll enjoy it?

Jack Maybe not. But the speakers will _____ ___ to you some things you never thought of.

Bob __ ___ ___, Jack, isn't your girlfriend one of the speakers?

Jack Yes, she is. She says that a man's place is in the home; ____ __, *he* should do the housework.

SUBSTITUTING

Replace boldface words with appropriate idioms. Then copy or repeat aloud the whole sentence in the correct tense and person.

1. Sam **mentioned** all the difficulties. ______________________________
____.

2. How many men **participated** in World War II? ______________________________
____?

3. **Allow me to think.** Where's my key? ______________________________
____?

4. I enjoyed the party; I **might add**, I met your boyfriend there. ______________

____.

5. My uncle's a big man; **to say it in another way**, he's more than six feet tall. ________

____.

CHOOSING

Write or say the appropriate idiom.

Mimi Did Japan ____________________ the Olympic games last summer?

Sam ____________________ if I can remember. No it didn't.

Mimi ____________________, my brother once belonged to France's Olympic swimming team.

Sam Wow! He must be a really good swimmer— ____________________, one of the best in France.

Mimi Yes, he is. I love to ____________________ it ____________________ to people. It makes me feel proud.

COMPLETING

that is • by the way • let . . . see • point out • take part in

Give the appropriate idiom. Then finish the sentence in your own words, using the correct tense and person.

1. John worked hard on his English. ____________________, his brother has _.

2. Emily was really fat; ____________________, she weighed _.

3. What should I wear to the play tonight? ____________________, should I _.

4. Andy loves sports. He has ____________________ many _.

5. Our mechanic has ____________________ why our car _.

CONTEXTUALIZING

In your own words, write (or tell) a story. Include four idioms from this lesson and use the ideas below. (60 to 85 words)

1) Bob and Ruby were an old married couple. 2) They had been married for thirty years. 3) They went everywhere together. 4) They did everything together. 5) They decided everything together. 6) It was a perfect marriage except for one thing. 7) Bob hated Ruby. 8) Ruby hated Bob.

VALUING

Discuss (write about) your viewpoint, using your idioms.

A. How do you feel about people emigrating from your country? 1) No one should leave permanently. It is the duty of a citizen to stay and help. 2) A few—for reasons of religion, politics, or personal choice—can leave. 3) A large number can leave. If people are unhappy, they make others around them unhappy. 4) Anyone should be able to leave. Restrictions on people's departure, temporary or permanent, violate their personal freedom.

B. Are there countries which forbid, or make it difficult, for their citizens to emigrate? Which ones? Why do you suppose these countries are against emigration?

Colorful saying: Far-out. Very different from other persons or things. Odd, unusual.

Lesson 18

AMERICANS GO SHOPPING

ROLE PLAYING

Sam We **took up** an interesting topic in psych* class yesterday: Why do Americans buy more than they need?

Mimi I know! Because they're stupid.

Sam Well, anyway a scientist secretly filmed supermarket shoppers as they **picked up** packages, cans, and bottles and put them in their shopping carts. After a while, their eyes were blinking at only half the normal rate. All the brightly colored labels seemed to be hypnotizing them.

Mimi How strange!

Sam But finally the time came to pay. **All at once** the shoppers began to blink faster and faster. When they saw the cash register, their blinking **went up** to 20 blinks a minute. They looked worried.

Mimi They had put too many things in their shopping carts and they were afraid they couldn't pay for them.

Sam How did you guess?

Mimi The supermarket **got the better of** me, too. I had to return half my groceries last week.

**Psych*—short for psychology. Informal student usage.

IDIOM CHECK

take up /S/ a) Begin to do, learn, or interest yourself in a topic, subject, job, sport, etc. *Mary took up teaching as her life's work./ At dinner we took up an interesting topic. We discussed the men's liberation movement.* b) Occupy time or space. *That table takes up too much space.*

pick up /S/ Gather, collect; obtain. Involves lifting and actions related to it, concretely or abstractly. *Your room is a mess. Please pick up your clothes and hang them in the closet. Could you pick up some beer for me at the supermarket? You could pick up bad habits from Mimi.* (Such as smoking too many cigarettes.)

all at once Suddenly; unexpectedly; without warning. *The storm got worse. Then all at once our lights failed.*

Equivalent: **all of a sudden.**

go up Increase; rise. *Every month our food prices go up.*

Compare: **stay the same.**
Contrast: **go down.**

get the better of Win against; beat; defeat. *Stay calm. Don't let your emotions get the better of your good sense. Yale often gets the better of Harvard in their annual football game.*

Equivalent: **get the best of.**

SPELLING

take up • pick up • all at once • go up • get the better of
Write or say the appropriate idiom. Use one letter for each blank.

Older people admit that they don't understand technology. It has _/_/_/_ _/_/_ _/_/_/_/_/_ _/_ them. But many young people have _/_/_/_/_ _/_ computer technology and learned to use their own computers. They can even _/_/_/_ _/_ an excellent one at a local department store. _/_/_ _/_ _/_/_/_ they've become "crazy" about computers. Unfortunately, tuition and prices of computer textbooks have _/_/_/_ _/_. The cost of education has doubled since 1974 in the U.S.

SUBSTITUTING

Replace boldface words with appropriate idioms. Then copy or repeat aloud the whole sentence in the correct tense and person.

1. Please **get** some stamps for me at the post office. ____.

2. **Suddenly** the ceiling fell on my head. ____.

3. I'll learn math! It won't **beat** me. ____.

4. I've **begun to learn** photography as a pastime. ____.

5. Food prices **increase** every month. ____

CHOOSING

Write or say the appropriate idiom.

Jane and Bill make quick decisions. Last year, ______________, they decided to ______________ tennis. I pointed out to them how difficult a game it would be to learn. But they wouldn't change their minds; they wouldn't let tennis ______________ of them. It cost them money, too—the cost of tennis equipment ______________ almost 100 percent last summer. But that didn't stop them: they ______________ some good secondhand equipment cheap and began playing.

COMPLETING

take up • pick up • all at once • go up • get the better of

Give the appropriate idiom. Then finish the sentence in your own words, using the correct tense and person.

1. If you listen to John, you might ______________ some new ideas about _.

2. ______________ the injured woman stopped breathing, but _.

3. Last Thursday our team ______________ the other team. We _.

4. I'm ______________ golf so that _.

5. If the cost of living ______________ any more, we'll _.

CONTEXTUALIZING

In your own words, write (or tell) a story. Include four idioms from this lesson and use the ideas below. (60 to 85 words)

1) Mimi went shopping every day. 2) She liked new clothes. 3) She often got dresses that she didn't need. 4) Without warning, her father began sending her less money. 5) "The cost of living is increasing," he said, "but not as fast as you spend my money." 6) Mimi has begun to make her own clothes.

VALUING

Discuss (write about) the cultures below, using your idioms.

A. Some cultures prize material advantages that come from science and industry. These cultures value a high standard of living. Other cultures center around personal and spiritual development—around man's relation to God and the universe. Your teacher will draw a line on the board with ENTIRELY SPIRITUAL marked as 1 and ENTIRELY MATERIAL marked as 10. Between these two *extremes*, where would you place the chief values of *your native country*? Make an *X* on the line at that point. Say why you put your *X* there.

B. Americans have often been called materialistic. Yet they give more money to charity than people of other countries and most of them attend religious services. How do you explain this contradiction?

Colorful saying: A rip-off (also a verb). A theft; action of exploitation.

Idiom Review of Lessons 16, 17, 18

Directions

a. Add letters to each circle so as to make an idiom.

b. Find the definition below that fits each idiom and put its *number* in the small circle.

c. Add the numbers in the circles across (→) or down (↓). The numbers *must* total 34. To help you start, one circle is already done.

Definitions

1. anticipate with pleasure
2. obtain; collect
3. defeat, win against
4. understand
5. omit
6. rise, increase
7. to say it more exactly
8. participate
9. by a great margin
10. continue
11. allow me to think
12. mention; direct someone's attention to
13. do something new
14. suggested by what is said; incidentally
15. suddenly; unexpectedly
16. investigate, examine

ONCE OVER LIGHTLY

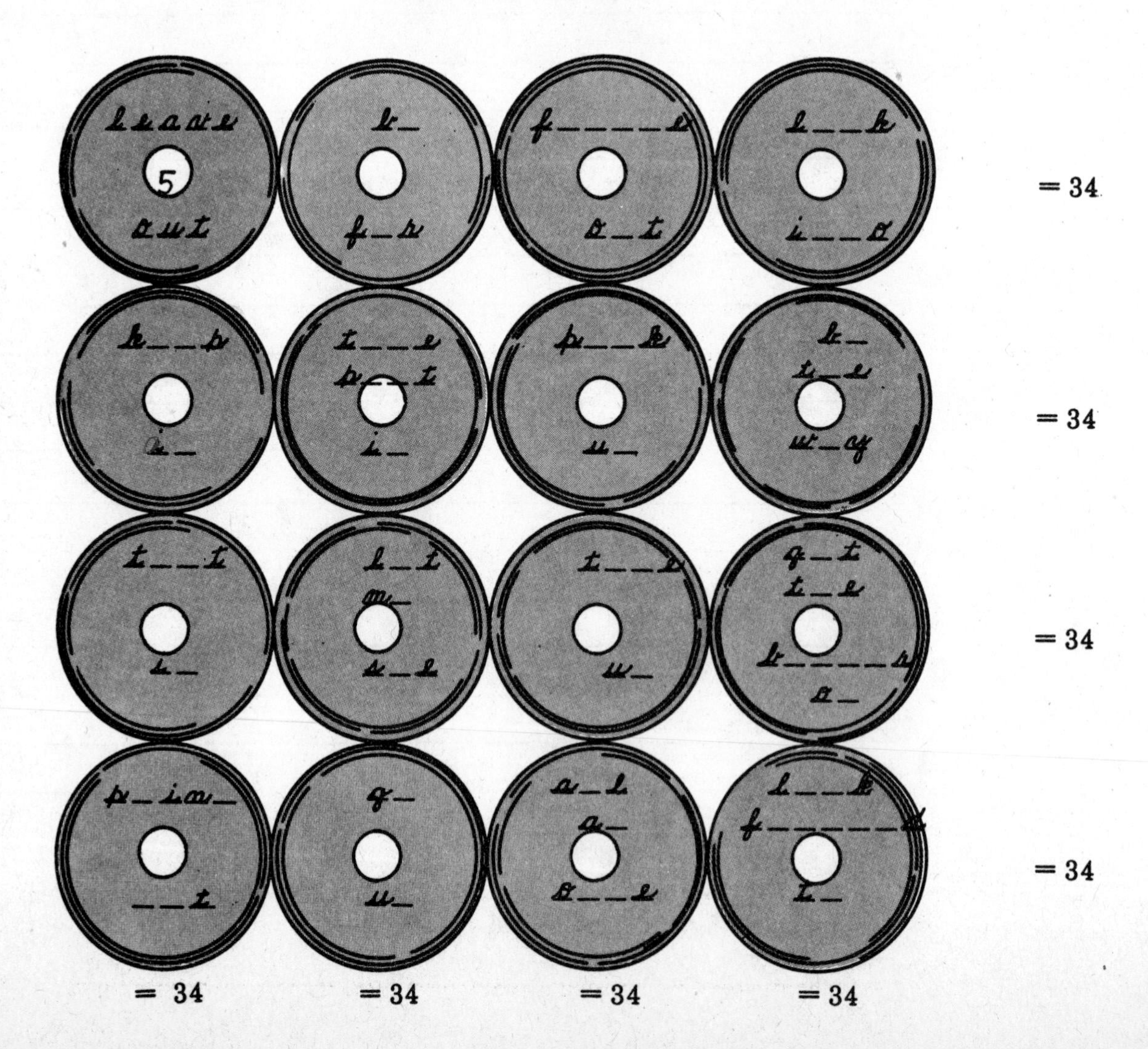

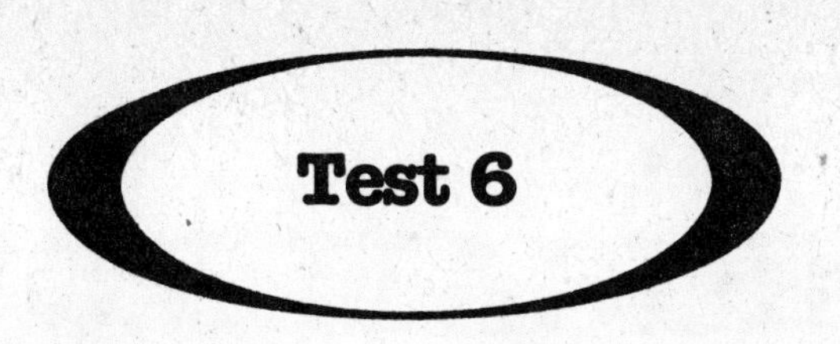

Test 6

Level I. From the **Completing** exercise of lessons 16, 17, 18, your teacher will choose five incomplete sentences and read them to you. Write them down, supply appropriate idioms for them, and finish them in your own words.

1 ______________________________

2 ______________________________

3 ______________________________

4 ______________________________

5 ______________________________

Level II. The pictures tell a story. In one paragraph of 90 to 120 words, tell this story or write it on a separate piece of paper. Include any five of these idioms: **figure out / by far / take part in / look at / by the way / take up / more and more / up to / all of a sudden**

Lesson 19

AMERICAN HOUSES: TOO MUCH ALIKE?

ROLE PLAYING

Mimi American houses—how surprising! They really look alike?

Sam Can't you **tell** red houses **from** green houses?

Mimi Idiot! Do you think **it's a question of** color? **No matter** what color they paint them, Americans build their houses the same.

Sam You're in a bad mood.

Mimi Maybe I am. So just **let** me **alone** and listen.

Sam Okay, okay.

Mimi In American towns, most houses are made of wood—that helps make them look alike—and at least 30 percent are ranch houses. Because ranch houses have only one story, they are **not much of** a house to look at.

Sam I rather like them.

Mimi You would!

IDIOM CHECK

tell somebody (thing) **from** somebody (thing) else. Recognize the difference; distinguish between. *I know nothing about wines. I can't tell a California wine from a French one.*

it is a question of It concerns; it is related to. *You shouldn't lie to your friends. It's a question of morality.*

no matter It makes no difference; regardless. *He'll become rich, no matter how many people he hurts to do it.*

let somebody (thing) **alone** Allow to be undisturbed; stay away from. *When Claudia gets angry, just let her alone. Don't even look at her./ Let the dog along or it will bite you.*

Equivalent: **leave . . . alone.**

not much of Not good; not important or significant. *Mona was always failing her tests; she was not much of a student. I only need a dollar; that's not much of a loan.*

SPELLING

tell from • it is a question of • no matter • not much of
Write or say the appropriate idiom. Use one letter for each blank.

Women must help one another: _/_ _/_ _ _/_/_/_/_/_/_/_ _/_ principle. _/_ _/_/_/_/_/_ what we women feel about other women personally, we are all sisters. However, we are also individuals. In a hundred ways, we can _/_/_/_ one woman _/_/_/_ another. If men will only _/_/_ us _/_/_/_/_, we can develop our individuality. It's _/_/_ _/_/_/_ _/_ a favor to ask them.

SUBSTITUTING

Replace boldface words with appropriate idioms. Then copy or repeat aloud the whole sentence in the correct tense and person.

1. Can you **recognize the difference between** real money **and** fake? ______________________________?
2. I'm busy. **Allow** me **to be undisturbed.** ______________________________.
3. **It made no difference** how nice I was, she always criticized me. ______________________________.
4. No wine; not much food; it was **not a good** party. ______________________________.
5. Here's why we can't travel this summer: It **isn't related to** money; it **is related to** time. ______________________________.

CHOOSING

Write or say the appropriate idiom.

When I was young, no one cheated or stole: ____________ simple honesty. ____________ how poor someone might be, he was never dishonest. Otherwise, people stayed away from him; they ____________.

Today stealing is like a second job for many people. For them, stealing a few dollars is ____________ a crime. Why? Because they cannot ____________ right ____________ wrong.

COMPLETING

tell from • it is a question of • no matter • let alone • not much of

Give the appropriate idiom. Then finish the sentence in your own words, using the correct tense and person.

1. It hasn't been ____________ vacation for me. First, it rained. Then ____________.
2. If you can't ____________ left ____________ right, you'll never become ____________.
3. Those kids must ____________ the dog ____________ or it ____________.
4. ____________ what Mimi tried to do, Sam ____________.
5. Joe wasn't able to come to the party. It ____________ his ____________.

CONTEXTUALIZING

In your own words, write (or tell) a story. Include four idioms from this lesson and use the ideas below. (60 to 85 words)

1) Sam wanted to rent a new apartment. 2) He had visited dozens. 3) He always found something wrong. 4) The rent was too high. 5) The ceilings were too low. 6) The landlady talked too much and disturbed him. 7) Perhaps Sam didn't know the difference between good and bad apartments. 8) Perhaps he was a bad judge. 9) Mimi finally chose Sam's apartment for him.

VALUING

Discuss (write about) houses in your native country, using your idioms.

A. Think of a typical house (or apartment) in your native country. What material is it usually made of? What color is it outside? Does it have many or few windows? Does it have no walls, low walls, or high walls around it? Can you describe the inside: furniture, rugs, decorations? Are rooms used for only one purpose or do they have different purposes? How does housing in your country express the needs and customs of your people?

B. Can you guess something about American needs and values from the way Americans build their houses?

Colorful saying: On the house. When the owner of a bar, hotel, or restaurant pays part or all of the bill.

Lesson 20

WOULD MIMI KILL SAM? WOULD SAM KILL MIMI?

ROLE PLAYING

Sam Were you really angry with me?

Mimi Yes, I was. After what **took place** at Bill's party, I felt like cutting you into pieces and selling you as dog food.

Sam I **might as well** admit it—I felt the same way.

Mimi What changed your mind?

Sam I **came to** realize that—that we were both wrong.

Mimi So did I. I was **about to** phone you last night.

Sam Me, too. I was even going to **ask** you **for** a date.

Mimi I accept!

IDIOM CHECK

ask for /S/ Request something; ask to be given something—used for addressing human beings and sometimes computers. *I asked my brother for* $5. Negative meaning: Behave so as to invite trouble. *If you drive while you're drunk, you're asking for trouble.*

Compare: **ask after; ask about.**

about to Ready to; on the point of doing something—some form of *be* precedes idiom; base form of verb follows it. *When the phone rang, Ed* **was** *about to* **leave.**/ *I like to smoke and I* **am** *not about to* **quit.** (I'm not going to quit smoking.)

take place Happen—suggests a planned event. *The wedding will take place at my house.*

Compare: **go on** (a continuing action).

might as well It seems reasonable; it seems preferable. *It's starting to rain; we might as well stay home.* (Because of the rain, it seems preferable to stay at home.)/ *You might as well admit it. I saw you do it.* (Because I saw you do it, why not be reasonable and admit it?)

Equivalent: **may as well.**

come to Acquire enough familiarity or understanding; learn to; grow to—never in continuous tense; followed by base form of verb. *After eating hamburgers every night for a year, I have come to* **hate** *them./ Once I really knew Sally, I came to* **love** *her.*

SPELLING

ask for • about to • take place • might as well • come to
Write or say the appropriate idiom. Use one letter for each blank.

On the highways of America, accidents _/_/_/_ _/_/_/_/_ every minute. At this very moment, an accident is _/_/_/_/_ _/_ happen. On the whole, however, most Americans drive within the speed limit. They _/_/_/_ _/_/_/_ _/_ realize that speed means injury and death and that they _/_/_/_/_/_ _/_ _/_/_/_ drive slowly and arrive safely. That's why many Americans _/_/_ _/_/_/_/_/_ _/_/_ stronger laws against speeding.

SUBSTITUTING

Replace boldface words with appropriate idioms. Then copy or repeat aloud the whole sentence in the correct tense and person.

1. His wife has **requested** a divorce. ____.
2. When Sam phoned, Mimi was **ready to** cry. ____.
3. What **happened** in English class today? A test? ____?
4. It took him a whole year, but Frank **learned to** like Arabic. ____.
5. Since nobody believes me anyway, **it would be reasonable for me to** lie. ____.

CHOOSING

Write or say the appropriate idiom.

Yesterday I ____________________ my boss ____________________ a raise in pay. "I ____________________ the conclusion," I told him, "that without $20 more a week, I ____________________ find another job."

At 5 p.m., when I was ____________________ stop work for the day, my boss invited me to his office. Believe me, I was surprised by what ____________________ there. I didn't get my raise; I was fired.

COMPLETING

ask for • about to • take place • might as well • come to

Give the appropriate idiom. Then finish the sentence in your own words, using the correct tense and person.

1. When Sam arrived, were you ____________________ phone Jim and _ ?

2. Carol is tired. She has ____________________ enough time off her job to _ .

3. I've ____________________ a decision about _ .

4. Most crimes have ____________________ in cities because _ .

5. Since Mimi had nothing to do last night, she ____________________ have _ .

CONTEXTUALIZING

In your own words, write (or tell) a story. Include four idioms from this lesson and use the ideas below. (60 to 85 words)

1) Boys want to date Maria. 2) They must always get permission from her parents first. 3) Maria's father decides whether or not she can have a date. 4) He usually says yes. 5) When he says no, Maria is ready to cry. 6) Sometimes she argues with him. 7) It would be more reasonable if she stayed calm. 8) She always loses the argument.

VALUING

Discuss (write about) this murder case, using your idioms.

A. Pat discovers that his wife Sue is "seeing" another man. Not only does she admit it, but she says that she isn't sorry. There is a loud, violent argument. Later that night neighbors hear three shots. When the police come, Sue claims that she has grabbed Pat's gun from him and shot him in self-defense. There are no eyewitnesses. Supposing you are the judge, what judgment do you make? 1) Execution? 2) Life imprisonment? 3) 10 to 20 years? 4) 1 to 10 years? 5) Acquittal—Sue goes free? State your reasons.

B. If Pat is the unfaithful partner and Sue is the one killed, do you make the same judgment? Why? Why not?

C. On a scale of 1 (anger should be openly, even physically expressed) to 7 (disagreements should always be calmly discussed), what place does anger have in your culture? How is it expressed? Not expressed? Why?

Colorful saying: Drive someone up the wall. Confuse, irritate, or anger a person so much that he or she becomes almost crazy.

Lesson 21

AMERICA AND THE RACE PROBLEM

ROLE PLAYING

Mimi Why does America have a race problem?

Sam Because different races live here.

Mimi Sam, **once and for all**, be serious.

Sam But I am serious. A one-race country doesn't have race problems: England's race problems didn't start until a million people from Africa and Asia came to live there. Then, in 1962, London and Birmingham had their first race riots.

Mimi Maybe that explains *why* there's a race problem here, but it doesn't excuse the U.S.

Sam Of course not. But racism is an old problem. **As yet**, no nation has completely solved it.

Mimi **Even so**, isn't the U.S. terribly racist?

Sam Some Americans are racists—yes. But all races are legally equal. In most places, Americans of every race now go to the same schools, work at the same jobs for the same pay, and often attend the same churches. Since World War II, different races have begun living in the same neighborhoods. So, you see, **step by step** America has been moving toward racial equality.

Mimi I also see that our waiter is white and the restaurant manager is black. Maybe you're right. **All in all**, there is more equality than I expected.

IDIOM CHECK

once and for all Finally; permanently; conclusively. *Dan decided to quit smoking once and for all.*

as yet Until now, until then—used with negation and negatively intended sentences. *It is midnight and my son has* **not** *come home as yet.* (As of midnight, he has not come home.)/ *As yet, there is* **no** *cure for the common cold.* (Up to the present, there is still no cure.)

even so However; although it is true. *Our hallway was dark; even so, I could see someone coming.* (Despite our hallway's being dark, I could see someone coming.)/ *All the students liked Bill. Even so, they elected Mary class president.* (Although it was true that all the students liked Bill, they elected Mary class president.)

Synonym: **just the same.**

step by step Gradually; by degrees; by consecutive parts. *Our chemistry professor described the process step by step./ We will win our freedom step by step.*

all in all In summary; everything counted. *You have two apples and I have three. All in all, that makes five./ All in all, I have little to complain about: I have money, free time, and good friends.*

Equivalent: **in all.**

SPELLING

once and for all • as yet • even so • step by step • all in all
Write or say the appropriate idiom. Use one letter for each blank.

I wanted to master English _/_/_/_ _/_/_ _/_/_ _/_/_. I had been studying it for nine months, but _/_ _/_/_ I didn't know all the irregular verbs. _/_/_/_ _/_, I generally did well on grammar exams.

The months passed. Slowly, _/_/_/_ _/_ _/_/_/_, I mastered all the irregular verbs. At the end of my first year of English, I felt that, _/_/_ _/_ _/_/_, I could be proud of myself. I really knew my English.

SUBSTITUTING

Replace boldface words with appropriate idioms. Then copy or repeat aloud the whole sentence in the correct tense and person.

1. Has the world been progressing **by degrees** toward peace? ____________
____?

2. **Up to now**, my brother hasn't learned to play baseball. ____________
____.

3. **Everything considered**, a teacher uses many different skills. ____________
____.

4. George wanted to forget the past **permanently**. ____________
____.

5. Dr. Smith makes mistakes sometimes; **nevertheless**, he is an excellent teacher.
____
____.

CHOOSING

Write or say the appropriate idiom.

After a heart attack, Larry decided, finally, ____________, that he had to exercise regularly. But he was careful; he knew that only two months had passed since his attack and that he wasn't in good health ____________. ____________, he began walking a mile a day.

Months passed. Slowly, ____________, he got his strength back and became well. His doctor examined him carefully. ____________, Larry was in good health.

COMPLETING

once and for all • as yet • even so • step by step • all in all

Give the appropriate idiom. Then finish the sentence in your own words.

1. My son was told to return home before eleven. ____________, he decided not to ____________________.

2. ____________, no one has discovered a cure for the common cold or ____________________.

3. Can you do it? Can you, ____________, quit ____________________
____________________?

4. Bob has been learning ____________________ to __ __ __ __ __ __ __ __ __

__ .

5. The weather was clear and sunny. ____________________, the flight to Boston was pleasant and __ .

CONTEXTUALIZING

In your own words, write (or tell) a story. Include four idioms from this lesson and use the ideas below. (60 to 85 words)

1) Doris was married last month. 2) She wants to learn to cook. 3) She hasn't succeeded. 4) But she is trying hard. 5) She is gradually improving. 6) She has all the qualities of a good cook—her husband says so. 7) It is a month after their marriage. 8) He still cooks all the meals.

VALUING

Discuss (write about) the racial problem below, using your idioms.

A. Your sister loves a man of a different race and they want to marry. She comes to you for advice. You are not a racist and you know that he is a good, honest man. But you must think of her future happiness and what might happen to her and her children. On a scale of 1 (marry him) to 3 (marry him but live where no one knows you) to 5 (never see him again), make an X by the number that best indicates the kind of advice you would give. What are your reasons?

B. Would you give the same advice to your brother? Why? Why not?

C. How would you help stop racism in the United States?

Colorful saying: Black-and-white. Everything is either good or bad, right or wrong, with nothing in between. *(To Mimi, the world is very simple. She sees it as black-and-white: the good guys and the bad guys.)*

Idiom Review of Lessons 19, 20, 21

Directions

a. Add letters to each circle so as to make an idiom.

b. Find the definition below that fits each idiom and put its *number* in the small circle.

c. Add the numbers in the circles across (⟶) or down (↓). The numbers *must* total 34. To help you start, one circle is already done.

Definitions

1. altogether; everything counted
2. it concerns
3. participate
4. not to disturb or bother somebody
5. happen, occur
6. gradually
7. finally, decisively
8. rather bad
9. ready to, on the point of
10. regardless; not to be considered
11. up to this time
12. this choice may be slightly better
13. nevertheless; despite the contrary
14. recognize one thing as differing from another
15. learn to; grow to
16. try to get something by expressing a desire for it; request

ONCE MORE, WITH FEELING

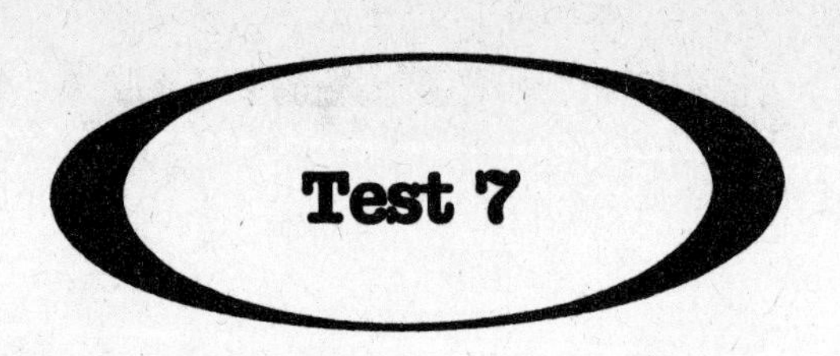

Test 7

Level I. From the **Completing** exercise of lessons 19, 20, 21, your teacher will choose five incomplete sentences and read them to you. Write them down, supply appropriate idioms for them, and finish them in your own words.

1 ______________________________

2 ______________________________

3 ______________________________

4 ______________________________

5 ______________________________

Level II. The pictures tell a story. In one paragraph of 90 to 120 words, tell this story or write it on a separate piece of paper. Include any five of these idioms: **it is a question of / not much of a / take place / about to / might as well / as long as / even so / as yet.**

Lesson 22

SAM DOESN'T PHONE

ROLE PLAYING

Mimi Why didn't you **call** me **up**? You said you would.

Sam I had to **go away** on business, so I didn't have much free time. Every time I **called up**, your phone was busy.

Mimi I thought you didn't phone **on purpose** . . . that you didn't want to talk to me.

Sam Suspicious woman!

Mimi Don't **make fun** of me. I even cried a little this afternoon.

Sam Really? Forgive me.

Mimi You knew **all along** I liked you.

Sam I—I like you, too.

IDIOM CHECK

all along Continuing from the start; during the whole time—with past and past perfect tenses only. *Smith was a great runner. I felt sure all along that he'd win.* (Even from the start, I felt that Smith would win.)/ *I pretended that I didn't recognize her, but all along I knew it was Emily.* (During the whole time I really knew who she was.)

Equivalent: **right along.**
Compare: **all the time.**

call up /S/ Telephone. *We called him up at the Hilton.*

Equivalent: **call.**

go away Depart; leave—but most often NOT permanently. *Don't go away; I have something to tell you.* (Don't leave my presence.)/ *He went away on vacation.* (He left here for his vacation.)

Contrast: **come back.**
Wrong: *He went away to Russia and lived there for ten years.*
Right: *He went to Russia and lived there for ten years.*

make fun of Laugh at; ridicule; tease. *Sam became angry when Mimi made fun of his short haircut.*

Equivalent (informal): **poke fun at.**

on purpose Intentionally; for a reason. *The clown fell down on purpose; he wanted to make the children laugh.* (The clown intentionally fell down.)

Contrast: **by accident.**
Wrong: *I did my homework on purpose.*
Right. *I did my homework.*
(Explanation: many verbs, such as *do,* include purpose in their meaning. That is why you cannot add *on purpose.*)

SPELLING

all along • call up • go away • make fun of • on purpose
Write or say the appropriate idiom. Use one letter for each blank.

Mimi cried last week when Sam _/_/_/_ _/_/_/_ to Miami. Of course, he _/_/_/_/_/_ _/_/_ _/_ the minute he arrived. She was pleased to hear him say he loved her although she had known it _/_/_ _/_/_/_/_. She knew, too, that he wouldn't hurt her _/_ _/_/_/_/_/_/_. Even so, she wanted to make him feel guilty for leaving her. But Sam guessed Mimi's little "game" and _/_/_/_ _/_/_ _/_ her.

SUBSTITUTING

Replace boldface words with appropriate idioms. Then copy or repeat aloud the whole sentence in the correct tense and person.

1. They had intended **even from the start** to go with us. ______________________
____.

2. Her boss **telephoned** her at 7 a.m. ______________________
____.

3. His wife had **left** on a boat trip. ______________________
____.

4. Was it an accident or did she break those dishes **for a reason**? ____________
____?

5. Please don't **laugh at** me; I hate it. ______________________
____.

CHOOSING

Write or say the appropriate idiom.

At midnight Dave's phone rang. It was his ex-girlfriend ____________. He had been afraid ____________ that she would do so. In fact, he had been very happy when she ____________ on a long vacation. When he answered the phone pleasantly, she laughed and ____________ him, so he knew that she was trying to hurt him ____________.

COMPLETING

all along • call up • go away • make fun of • on purpose

Give the appropriate idiom. Then finish the sentence in your own words.

1. Mimi didn't hang up by accident. She did it ____________ because _.
2. Dave has ____________ on a long trip and _.
3. Sam didn't like Mimi's new dress. He ____________ it because _.
4. If I had ____________ my parents earlier and said where I was, they _.
5. My teacher had known ____________ that _.

CONTEXTUALIZING

In your own words, write (or tell) a story. Include four idioms from this lesson and use the ideas below. (60 to 85 words)

1) Sam sometimes teases Mimi. 2) Mimi is not used to being teased. 3) Now Mimi teases Sam. 4) He knows that she isn't serious. 5) Nevertheless, he sometimes becomes angry. 6) He won't phone Mimi for two or three days. 7) Sometimes she won't phone him either. 8) Maybe they are both being silly?

VALUING

Discuss (write about) teasing, using your idioms.

A. In your native country, do people sometimes tease you? Do you tease them? Are there people you must not tease? Why?

B. How do you tease a person? With words? Facial exprssions? Gestures? In other ways? On a scale of 1 (no one does it) to 7 (everybody does it), try to rate the importance of teasing in your culture. Why is (or isn't) it important?

C. In America, people often tease one another. Is it done gently or cruelly? Is it sometimes done to make the person relax? Does it mean that she or he has been accepted into the group?

D. If your teacher is an American, does she or he ever tease you? Yes? No? In what ways? Why?

Colorful saying: A hang-up. (A) An obstacle or delay. (B) An inhibition or nervous reaction to some situation.

Lesson 23

RELIGION IN AMERICA: SOME FACTS

ROLE PLAYING

Sam This whole week I've been **reading up on** religion in America. I've finished three books on the subject.

Mimi That's curious. I've just now **looked up** a lot of facts myself. Did you know that the United States has twice as many Jews—

Sam As Israel.

Mimi That it has more Catholics than—

Sam France.

Mimi As for Protestants—

Sam There are 86,000,000 of them and they belong to over 200 denominations.

Mimi Besides the Bu—

Sam Buddhists, Moslems, and Hindus, there are about 5,000,000 Orthodox Christians.

Mimi You win! I'm **calling off** the contest.

Sam But I'm not finished. **Keep quiet** and listen. Did you know that only two religions are native to the United States—Christian Science and Mormonism? Did you know—

Mimi No, I didn't know you **had in mind** becoming my teacher. I feel like I'm at school.

IDIOM CHECK

read up on Study a subject in general in order to prepare yourself for a test, interview, discussion, etc.; study by doing extra reading. *Before taking your economics exam, you had better read up on savings and loans./ I read up on* Moby Dick *yesterday.* (Meaning you studied articles and books *about* Melville's great novel.)/ *I read* Moby Dick *yesterday.* (Meaning you read the novel itself.)

look up /S/ Search for specific information in a phone book, dictionary, encyclopedia, etc.; do research for particular information. *Sam looks up difficult words in his dictionary./ John's full name is John B. Smith. Please look up his phone number for me.*

call off /S/ Cancel; decide against doing something already planned. *It was raining, so we called off the picnic.*

keep quiet /S/ a) Don't speak or make noise (being a command, this idiom may be impolite; it is never used with bosses, teachers, older people, and strangers.) *Keep quiet! I'm trying to write a letter.*

Compare: **shut up.**

b) To remain silent. *If good men keep quiet, evil men will succeed.*

Contrast: **speak out.**

have in mind /S/ + either infinitive or gerund Intend; plan. *What did you have in mind doING (to do) tonight?*

Compare: **have a (good) mind to.**

SPELLING

read up on • look up • call off • keep quiet • have in mind
Write or say the appropriate idiom. Use one letter for each blank.

William had been a good history student. He had listened carefully to his teacher, written many notes, and _/_/_/_ _/_/_/_/_ in class. In the month before his final exam, he _/_/_ _/_/_/_ _/_ _/_ two hundred years of American history and he _/_/_ _/_/_/_/_/_ _/_ in an almanac the names of all the states and their capitals. He _/_/_ even _/_/_/_/_/_ _/_/_ his dates with his girlfriend so that he could study every night.

What was William's intention? Obviously he _/_/_ _/_ _/_/_/_ to be first in his class.

SUBSTITUTING

Replace boldface words with appropriate idioms. Then copy or repeat aloud the whole sentence in the correct tense and person.

1. Did the salesman **search for** the prices for you? ______________________

   ____?
2. For a long time I've **planned** a trip around the world. ______________________

   ____.
3. We had **remained silent** until our teacher asked our opinion. ______________

   ____.
4. Because he felt sick, my father **canceled** his trip. ______________________

   ____.
5. I had **studied** the culture of the Incas before I went to the museum. ________

   ____.

CHOOSING

Write or say the appropriate idiom.

After he failed his history test, Joe learned that he ______________ the wrong dates and that he ______________ the wrong century. But it was his own fault: If he ______________ instead of talking, he would have passed the test. However, he had thought very little about history, for he ______________ getting acquainted with the pretty girl sitting beside him. He had even phoned Professor Smith and ______________ an office appointment with him so that he could meet the girl downtown.

COMPLETING

read up on • look up • call off • keep quiet • have in mind
Give the appropriate idiom. Then finish the sentence in your own words.

1. Half the players were sick, so our football coach had ______________ our game rather than _.
2. Did Donna ______________ the spelling of "Mississippi" in a dictionary or _.
3. My father was angry. That's why I ______________ while he _.

4. My friends wanted to go to a movie, but I ____________________ a(n) _ _ _ _

_ .

5. Ruth had studied math and ____________________ computer technology because she wanted _ .

CONTEXTUALIZING

In your own words, write (or tell) a story. Include four idioms from this lesson and use the ideas below. (60 to 85 words)

1) Americans love baseball. 2) From April to early October they read the sports pages of their newspapers. 3) They study the "statistics" of how well their team plays. 4) The children must not make any noise while their father watches baseball on TV. 5) Sometimes a game is canceled because of bad weather. 6) Then many Americans don't know how to amuse themselves. 7) They visit neighbors to talk about baseball.

VALUING

Discuss (write about) the role of religion in your country, using your idioms.

A. How big a role does religion (attending religious services, observing religious holidays, obeying religious laws, using religion as a means of government) have in the life of your country? On a scale of 1 (no role at all) to 10 (everything done relates to religion), rate the role you think it has. Give examples.

B. The United States government leaves its people free to practice *any* religion. It also leaves them free to neither practice nor believe in religion. Do you think this separation of religion and the state is good or bad? Why?

Colorful saying: Jesus freak. Somebody who practices his or her religion (Christianity) excessively and showily.

Lesson 24

DO AMERICANS LIKE THEIR NEIGHBORS?

ROLE PLAYING

Mimi Sam, **let go of** my hand! I want to point at something.

Sam Okay, but I want a kiss for **giving** it **back** to you.

Mimi You're an idiot!

Sam If that's the way you feel . . .

Mimi And don't look hurt. Just answer me: What makes all those houses look alike?

Sam **Every other** one has a two-car garage?

Mimi No. Look at the lawns. What do you see?

Sam Grass.

Mimi What else?

Sam I give up. I've **run out of** ideas.

Mimi You're not trying. Can't you see that only one of those houses has a fence around it? In France our houses often have big fences or walls around them. Sometimes we stick broken glass on top of our walls.

Sam For years I've been trying to **make out** why the French differ from other people. Now I know! The French don't like each other.

IDIOM CHECK

let go (of) Release; stop holding something or somebody. *Let go of him! He's not the man who stole your money.*

Contrast: **hold onto.**

give back /S/ Return something to somebody. *Jack didn't want to give me back my pen.*

every other + singular noun Alternate. *Arlene works Tuesday, Thursday, and Saturday—that is, she works every other day.*

run out of Use all of something; exhaust it. *Has your car enough gas? You don't want to run out of gas on the highway.*

make out /S/ See, hear, interpret, understand someone or something. *I can't make out what Sam is saying. He doesn't speak clearly./ In the fog, it's hard to make out street signs./ I could never make out what Aristotle meant. His ideas were too difficult.*

SPELLING

let go (of) • give back • every other • run out of • make out
Write or say the appropriate idiom. Use one letter for each blank.

_/_/_/_/_ _/_/_/_/_ night Sam and Mimi went to the movies. In the dark, they held hands. Whenever Mimi _/_/_ _/_ of Sam's hand, he felt a little sad. By her smile, however, he _/_/_/_ _/_/_ that she wasn't angry at him.

But how could she be angry? She still owed him ten dollars. In fact, every time she _/_/_ _/_/_ _/_ money, she borrowed from Sam. Of course, she _/_/_/_ his money _/_/_/_ to him a few days later.

SUBSTITUTING

Replace boldface words with appropriate idioms. Then copy or repeat aloud the whole sentence in the correct tense and person.

1. Have you **completely used your supply of** notebook paper? ____?
2. **Stop holding** my suitcase; I can carry it. ____.
3. Can you **understand** Dr. Smith's handwriting? ____?
4. **Return** it to me! ____!
5. *Biennial* means happening on **alternate** year(s). ____.

CHOOSING

Write or say the appropriate idiom.

Marge invited Herman to dinner twice a month. The last time she invited him he accidentally __________ a beautiful vase and it broke on the floor. He had tried to excuse himself, but he soon __________ words.

The following day he bought another vase. Of course, he could not __________ Marge __________ a vase *exactly* like the one he broke, but he found one that looked so much like the old one that she could hardly __________ any difference.

When Marge received it, she thanked him. Naturally she kept inviting him to dinner __________ week.

COMPLETING

let go (of) • give back • every other • run out of • make out

Give the appropriate idiom. Then finish the sentence in your own words.

1. When his class __________ time and couldn't finish their exam, Dr. Smith told them _.
2. If your boyfriend borrows your car, he should __________ to you _.
3. The mailman stopped at __________ house because _.
4. Have you __________ why _.
5. Don't __________ the steering wheel while _.

CONTEXTUALIZING

In your own words, write (or tell) a story. Include four idioms from this lesson and use the ideas below. (60 to 85 words)

1) Mimi had no class three mornings a week. 2) She and her landlady drank coffee together on those mornings. 3) Mimi told her what went on at school. 4) Her landlady talked about going to France. 5) They also talked about French and American culture and tried to see what the differences were. 6) Mimi's landlady loved to talk. 7) But Mimi had lots of patience and listened politely to everything she said.

VALUING

Discuss (write about) individualism, using your idioms.

A. In some nations, individuals matter more than society. They can justify their actions by merely saying, "That is the way we are." No additional explanation is necessary. In other nations, society matters more than any individual. These nations emphasize cooperation and group loyalty at the cost of individual freedom. On a scale of 1 (individual counts most) to 7 (society counts most), rank your native country. Give examples of what behavior it tolerates (public free speech?) and what it doesn't (homosexuality? divorce?)

B. Although most American houses have no walls around them, do *neighbors* enter without knocking? Come without an invitation but knock? Can they come without an invitation?

C. Apply the above questions to your neighbors back home.

Colorful saying: Let it all hang out. Reveal everything (good *and* bad) about yourself.

Idiom Review of Lessons 22, 23, 24

Directions

a. Add letters to each circle so as to make an idiom.

b. Find the definition below that fits each idiom and put its *number* in the small circle.

c. Add the numbers in the circles across (⟶) or down (↓). The numbers *must* total 34. To help you start, one circle is already done.

Definitions

1. every second one
2. understand
3. telephone
4. remain silent
5. study by reading about
6. return something
7. depart; leave
8. release
9. search for (in a book of reference)
10. cancel
11. from the beginning
12. come to the end of; exhaust your supply of
13. something done intentionally, not accidentally
14. have as a plan or purpose
15. not to bother or disturb somebody
16. laugh at; ridicule

THE SAME OLD TUNE

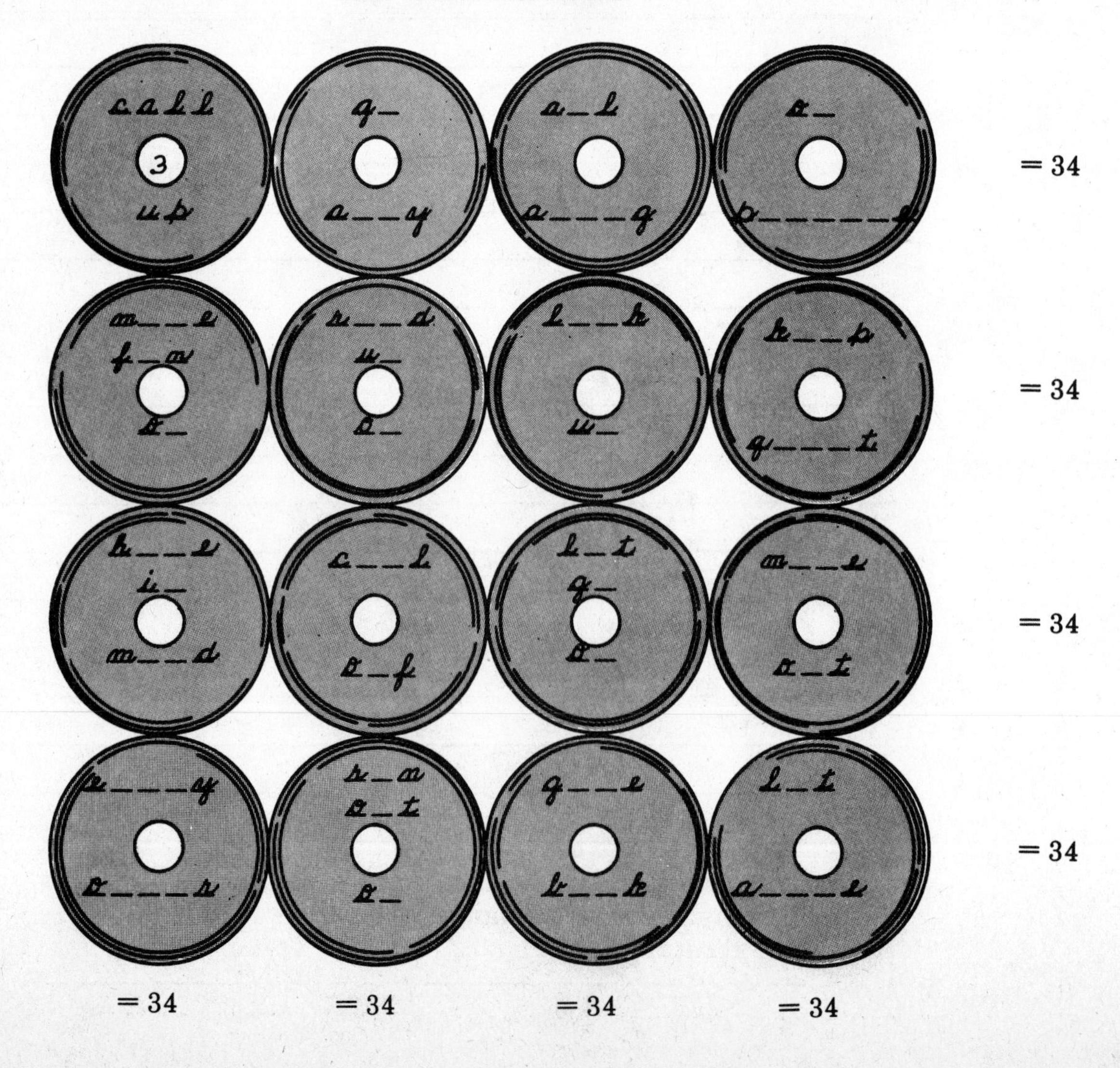

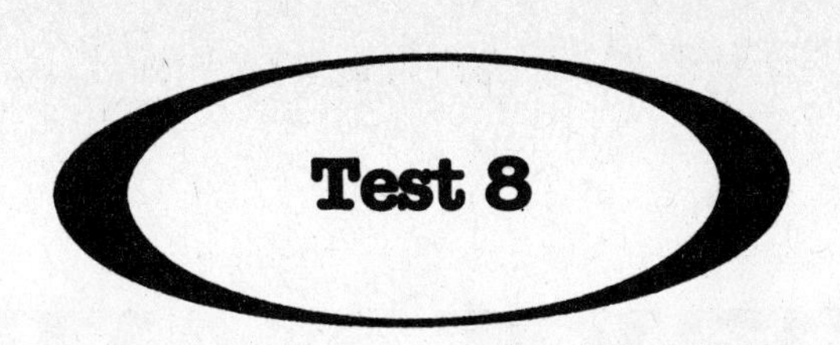

Test 8

Level I. From the **Completing** exercise of lessons 22, 23, 24, your teacher will choose five incomplete sentences and read them to you. Write them down, supply appropriate idioms for them, and finish them in your own words.

1 ______________________________

2 ______________________________

3 ______________________________

4 ______________________________

5 ______________________________

Level II. The pictures tell a story. In one paragraph of 100 to 130 words, tell this story or write it on a separate piece of paper. Include any five of these idioms: **go away / on purpose / keep quiet / have in mind / let go of / make out / give back**

Lesson 25

A SEXY HAIRDO

ROLE PLAYING

Sam Where were you? I've been **looking for** you.

Mimi I've **just now** gotten back. I've been shopping.

Sam I've bought two theater tickets. How about going to a play tonight?

Mimi I'd love to go. But first—tell me—have you noticed my hair? I **had** Jules **cut** it in a style I like.

Sam It certainly makes you look . . .

Mimi **Go ahead** and say it.

Sam Sexy.

Mimi Look sexy? I am sexy. I'm a Frenchwoman.

Sam **For once**, I agree with you.

IDIOM CHECK

look for Try to find; search for. *James looked for his keys, but he didn't see them anywhere./ Are you still looking for a job?*

Compare: **look up.**
Wrong: *I'll look up new furniture.*
Right: *I'll look for new furniture.*

just now A very short time ago; almost this minute. *Where's Mary? She was here just now.*

Compare: **right now.**
Contrast: **a long time before.**

have (someone) do, finish, make, accomplish, etc. (something) Cause a human being—but rarely an animal—to accomplish some act; the verb following *have* keeps its base form. *Have the dentist* **fix** *that tooth./ We had the landlord* **paint** *our house./ Mimi had Sam* **help** *her with irregular verbs./ Who had Joe* **clean** *the floor?*

go ahead Intransitive, often followed by *and* or by *with* or *on.* Proceed without hesitation; act quickly. *Go ahead* **and** *get dressed. We're late for the party./ Go ahead* **with** *your plan. It sounds good.*

for once This one time; on this occasion only. *Mother to son: I always tell you to do your homework but you never do it. For once do what I tell you.*

Equivalents: **for this once, just this once.**
Compare: **from time to time, half the time, most of the time.**

SPELLING

look for • just now • have (someone) do, finish, make, accomplish, etc. (something) • go ahead • for once
Write or say the appropriate idiom. Use one letter for each blank.

_/_/_ _/_/_/_, my wife and I agreed: We needed a new house. Since a good builder was a friend of ours, we told him to _/_ _/_/_/_/_ and build it. We _/_/_ _/_/_ _/_/_/_ it exactly as we wanted it built.

He has _/_/_/_ _/_/_ called up and told us our house is ready. For the next few weeks, I suppose, my wife and I will be _/_/_/_/_/_/_ _/_/_ new furniture.

SUBSTITUTING

Replace boldface words with appropriate idioms. Then copy or repeat aloud the whole sentence in the correct tense and person.

1. Did you **cause** Joe **to** paint your house? ______________________________
____?

2. (May I ask a question?) **Begin**. Ask it. ______________________________
____.

3. (Did you see John?) Yes, I saw him **a very short time ago.** __________________
____.

4. I've been **trying to find** you everywhere! ______________________________
____!

5. **This one time**, did you finish your homeowrk? ____________________________
____?

CHOOSING

Write or say the appropriate idiom.

My brother should do his own homework. Instead of ____________ a friend to help him, he should open his book, ____________, and do it himself. But he usually asks his girlfriend to do his work. He ____________ her ____________ it for him while he reads the newspaper.

But today, ____________, he found no one to do it for him. That didn't bother him; he went to see a movie. He has ____________ left the house.

COMPLETING

look for • just now • have (someone) do, finish, make, accomplish, etc. (something) • go ahead • for once

Give the appropriate idiom. Then finish the sentence in your own words.

1. (Someone must repair my car.) I have ____________ a mechanic ____________ my car so that _.
2. If you have work to do, just ____________ and start _.
3. A short time ago something terrible happened. I've heard ____________ that _.
4. Mary often lied, but ____________ she _.
5. John lost his wallet. He is ____________ everywhere and _.

CONTEXTUALIZING

In your own words, write (or tell) a story. Include four or five idioms from this lesson and use the ideas below. (75 to 90 words)

1) Mimi wears tight-fitting sweaters. 2) She also buys very tight pants. 3) Sam disapproves. 4) He says that it's wrong to dress that way. 5) Mimi wants to please him. 6) They visit his relatives. 7) She wears a loose sweater and a skirt.

VALUING

Discuss (write about) sexiness, using your idioms.

What makes a man or woman sexy? Good looks? Well-built body? Clothes and the "way" they are worn? Eye contact? Smiles? Gestures and body language? Other reasons?

Should a woman be allowed to look or act sexy? On a scale of 1 (actively discouraged) to 6 (actively encouraged), how does *your* culture react? What if the woman is married?

What about a man looking or acting sexy? What does your culture say about it?

Colorful saying: A hot dish. A woman who is considered very sexy.

Lesson 26

ARE AMERICANS INDIVIDUALISTS?

ROLE PLAYING

Mimi For a long time I thought Americans were conformists, but **at last** I've decided—by how they dress—that it isn't so. What do you say?

Sam I can't say. **Instead of** looking at clothes, I listen to conversations.

Mimi Even so, at the school play Friday night, you must have noticed the different skirts the girls were wearing: minis, midis, maxis. Two or three even **had on** evening gowns.

Sam Oh yes, now I remember. And did you notice the guys who came in blue jeans and bare feet?

Mimi Those horrible boys who couldn't tell a picnic from a play?

Sam You're not fair! It's what they prefer—being natural.

Mimi I **would rather** be unnatural.

Sam And beautiful!

Mimi Sam, you say the sweetest things. That's why we **get along** so well.

IDIOM CHECK

at last (also, **at long last**) After a long time; finally. *Everybody was getting worried, but Al came home at last./ At last we reached New York, but only after ten hours of driving.*

Contrast: **in a short time.**

instead of Rather than; in place of. *Instead of goING to a restaurant, we'll eat at home./ To a waiter: Give me cherry pie instead of apple pie.*

have on /S/ Be wearing—never used in continuous tense, although it suggests the continuous. *Mother: Does Joan have on her blue dress today? Joan's sister: Yes, she has it on. She's wearing it.*

would rather Do something willingly; do by choice; prefer—often followed by **than.** *Eric: Are you coming to the picnic with us? George: No, I'd rather not./ Mimi would rather eat meat* **than** *fish.*

get along (with) Be friendly or in harmony; agree on most things. *My parents get along well.* (They seldom fight or argue.)/ *Our neighbors don't speak to us and we don't speak to them. We don't get along with them.*

SPELLING

at last • instead of • have on • would rather • get along
Write or say the appropriate idiom. Use one letter for each blank.

For a long time Bruno had had trouble understanding American ways. That was why he _/_/_/_/_ _/_/_/_/_/_ be with other foreigners than with Americans. But I knew that _/_ _/_/_/_ he was able to _/_/_ _/_/_/_/_ with Americans when I saw him cheering and shouting at a Boston University basketball game. He _/_/_ _/_ a B.U. sweater and _/_/_/_/_/_/_ _/_ being with other foreigners, he was with American students.

SUBSTITUTING

Replace boldface words with appropriate idioms. Then copy or repeat aloud the whole sentence in the correct tense and person.

1. The plane flew ten hours. **Finally** it reached its destination. ______________________________.
2. I **prefer to** stay home tonight. ______________________________.
3. I **am wearing** my red shoes. ______________________________.
4. **Are you friendly** with your cousins? ______________________________.
5. I'll be visiting Cleveland **rather than** Philadelphia. ______________________________.

CHOOSING

Write or say the appropriate idiom.

__________________ going on dates and having a good time, Maria and Estella studied English every night last week. They had decided that they __________________ get a good grade than have fun.

But tonight they are going to a party and they __________________ pretty dresses. __________________, after all their studying, they are going to have some fun. They know that they will enjoy the party and __________________ with everyone there.

COMPLETING

at last • instead of • have on • would rather • get along

Give the appropriate idiom. Then finish the sentence in your own words.

1. Janet decided to walk to work__________________ taking _ .
2. If we had the choice, we __________________ eat steak than _ .
3. I__________________ my tennis shoes yesterday because _ .
4. Winter seemed to last forever, but__________________ spring _ .
5. I can __________________ with anyone except _ .

CONTEXTUALIZING

In your own words, write (or tell) a story. Include four or five idioms from this lesson and use the ideas below. (75 to 90 words)

1) Robert was careless. 2) He left his clothes on the bedroom floor. 3) It was easier to leave his clothes there than to hang them in a closet. 4) Sometimes he even wore right and left socks of different colors. 5) His wife criticized him constantly. 6) Finally, he tired of her criticism. 7) He wanted them to live in harmony. 8) Now he is careful about what he wears and where he wears it.

VALUING

Discuss (write about) women's liberation, using your idioms.

A. In some countries a woman's husband and parents decide what she should do, where she should go, whom she should meet, even what she should wear. In other countries, a very young woman can decide for herself many or all of these things. Imagine a scale of 1 to 10: 1 (everything decided for you) and 10 (you decide everything yourself). If you are a woman, where would you place yourself on this scale? Why? If you are a man, where would you place your countrywomen on this scale? For both men and women: Where do you think women *ought* to be on this scale—higher, lower, the same as they now are?

B. Many married and unmarried women—especially young ones—are very independent in thought and act. Discuss some of the advantages (to them and others) of this independence. What disadvantages might come from it?

C. What effect would (does) women's liberation have on your country?

Colorful saying: Do your (own) thing. Engage in an activity which completely suits and satisfies you.

Lesson 27

HOW MUCH IS TOO MUCH?

ROLE PLAYING

Mimi I'll have to **cut out** eating midnight snacks. I'm too fat.

Sam You don't look fat.

Mimi I'll turn sideways. Now **let** me **know** the truth.

Sam You've gained a pound or two. At the most. Maybe you could **do with** more exercise.

Mimi Exercise makes me hungry. Besides, I never **feel up to** exercising.

Sam Or you could **cut down on** your weight by eating fish. Fish isn't fattening.

Mimi I hate fish! I'd rather stop eating first.

Sam In Japan we like fish. We eat it all the time.

Mimi Oh!

IDIOM CHECK

cut out /S/ Stop doing; refrain from; omit—+ ING. *After he was sick, John cut out smokING and drinkING.*

let . . . know /obligatory S/ Inform; tell. *Let me know when you arrive in New York./ The doctor let Christine know that she needed an operation.*

do with Benefit from; find useful or helpful; need—modals *can, could, will, would, must,* etc. precede it. *After two years of hard work, I* **could** *do with a long vacation.*

Contrast: **do without.**

feel up to Be well enough to; feel able to + ING. *My girlfriend has a cold; she doesn't feel up to goING to school./ Debbie: How about going swimming? Maria: No thanks. I don't feel up to it.*

cut down on Reduce; lessen + ING. *We'll have to cut down on spendING or we'll be in trouble.*

Contrast: **go up on.**

SPELLING

cut out • let know • do with • feel up to • cut down on

Write or say the appropriate idiom. Use one letter for each blank.

Mimi has been worrying about her weight. The last few days she has been _/_/_/_/_/_/_ _/_/_ cake and candy entirely. It's all because Sam _/_/_ _/_/_ _/_/_/_ that she was getting fat. She could _/_ _/_/_/_ more exercise, but it makes her feel hungry. Afterward, she _/_/_/_ _/_ _/_ eating everything in the fridge instead of _/_/_/_/_/_/_ _/_/_/_ _/_ food.

SUBSTITUTING

Replace boldface words with appropriate idioms. Then copy or repeat aloud the whole sentence in the correct tense and person.

1. I could **benefit from** a good hot meal. ______________________________
______________________________.

2. I drink too much. I have to **reduce** my drinking. ______________________________
______________________________.

3. **Am I capable of** running ten miles today? Yes. ______________________________
______________________________.

4. When you land in Chicago, **inform** me. ______________________________
______________________________.

5. I was so nervous that I had to **stop** drinking coffee. ______________________________
______________________________.

CHOOSING

Write or say the appropriate idiom.

Paul's wife had told him that she'd rather he didn't smoke. His doctor had also ____________ that he shouldn't smoke.

Paul agreed with them. For years he had wanted to ____________ smoking completely, and recently he had ____________ it by 50 percent. But sometimes he didn't ____________ resisting a good smoke. So when he felt that he could ____________ a smoke, he went ahead and smoked.

COMPLETING

cut out • let know • do with • feel up to • cut down on

Give the appropriate idiom. Then finish the sentence in your own words.

1. After I had ____________ eating any candy, I _ .
2. Has Professor Smith ____________ you ____________ that _ ?
3. Bob looks very tired. Will he ____________ working _ ?
4. We had ____________ the amount of time we _ .
5. When people are in trouble, they can ____________ some help from _ .

CONTEXTUALIZING

In your own words, write (or tell) a story. Include four or five idioms from this lesson and use the ideas below. (75 to 90 words)

1) Paul smoked three packs of cigarettes a day. 2) He drank a quart of whiskey a day. 3) His doctor warned him of the dangers. 4) Paul stopped smoking entirely. 5) He drank only one small glass of whiskey after dinner. 6) Everybody told him how healthy he looked. 7) Paul himself thought that he was able to do anything—even run in a marathon.

VALUING

Discuss (write about) your opinion, using your idioms.

A. When Mrs. Jones married Mr. Jones, he was 5 feet 10 inches tall, weighed 160 pounds, and had a strong, muscular body. Ten years later he weighed 280 pounds. Mrs. Jones constantly asked him to lose weight. He always promised her to, but he never did. In fact, twelve years after they were married, he weighed 300 pounds. It was then that Mrs. Jones asked him for a divorce. (They had no children.)
How do you feel about her action? Would you feel the same if it were the other way around—Mrs. Jones fat, Mr. Jones asking for a divorce? Give reasons to defend your point of view.

B. Many Americans are overweight. Do you think it comes from the kind of food they eat? From TV ads which encourage eating and drinking? Other reasons plus the above?

Colorful saying: Eat like a horse. Eat a lot of food; have a big appetite.

Idiom Review of Lessons 25, 26, 27

Directions

a. Add letters to each circle so as to make an idiom.

b. Find the definition below that fits each idiom and put its *number* in the small circle.

c. Add the numbers in the circles across (⟶) or down (↓). The numbers *must* total 34. To help you start, one circle is already done.

Definitions

1. stop, suppress
2. begin immediately
3. be able to
4. be wearing
5. in place of; rather than
6. prefer
7. reduce; lessen
8. for one time
9. search for
10. make someone do something
11. use with advantage
12. finally, after a long time
13. intend; plan
14. a moment ago
15. inform
16. be friendly with

KEEPING THE MEMORY ALIVE

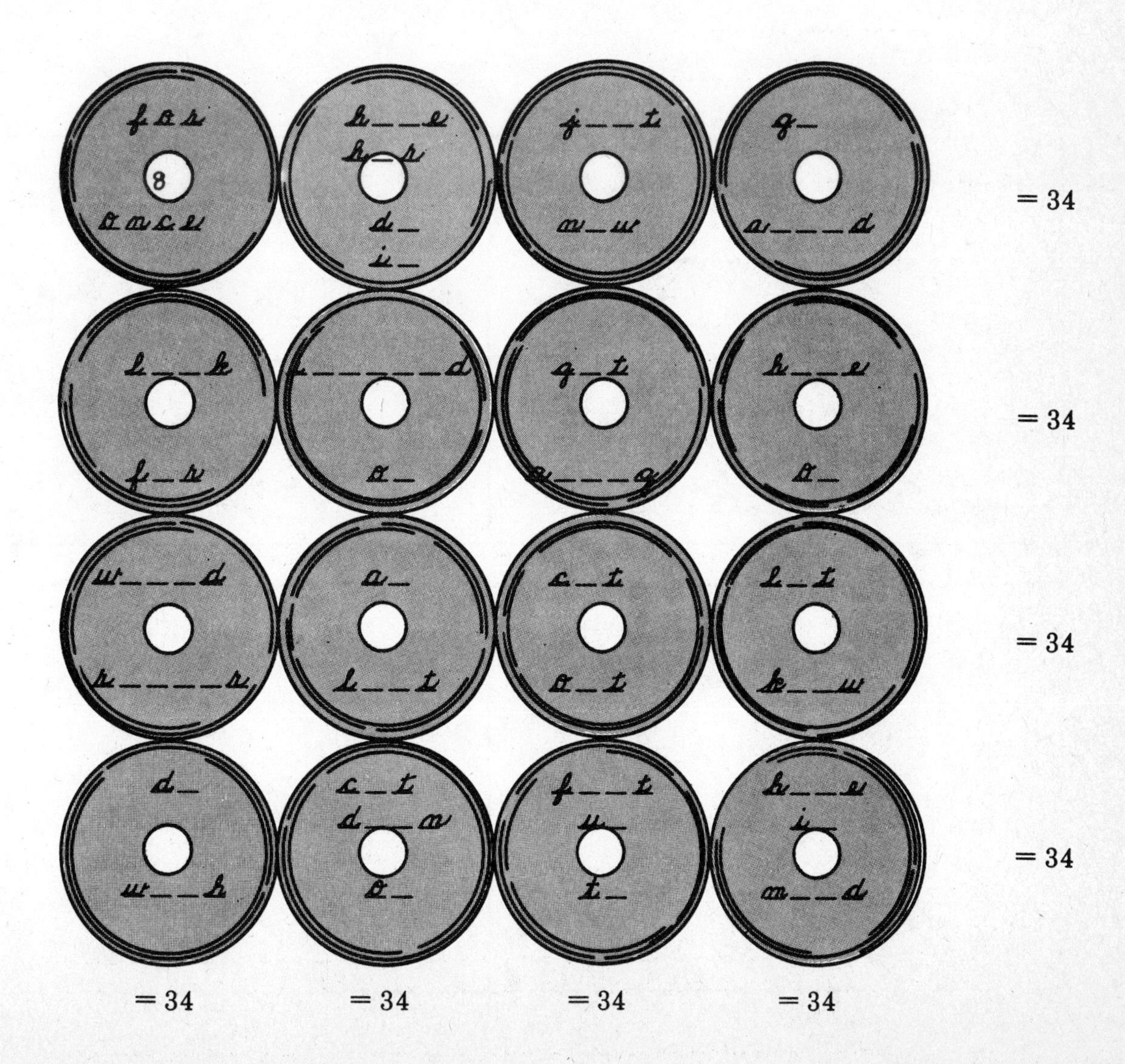

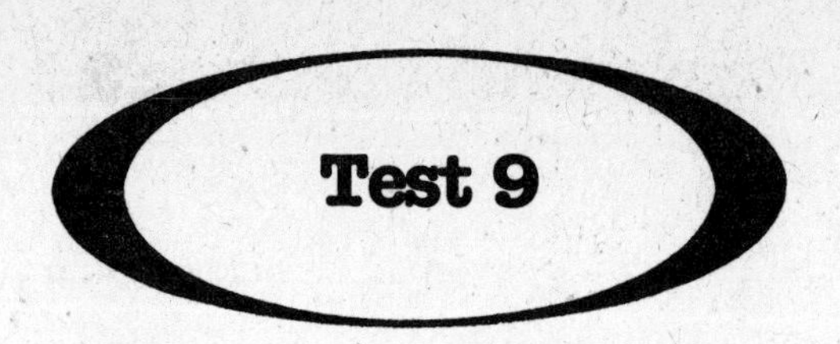

Test 9

Level I. From the **Completing** exercise of lessons 25, 26, 27, your teacher will choose five incomplete sentences and read them to you. Write them down, supply appropriate idioms for them, and finish them in your own words.

1 ____

2 ____

3 ____

4 ____

5 ____

Level II. The pictures tell a story. In one paragraph of 100 to 130 words, tell this story or write it on a separate piece of paper. Include any five of these idioms: **for once / look for / instead of / would rather / at last / do with**

Lesson 28

MIMI HAS A TOOTHACHE

ROLE PLAYING

Sam Mimi, what's the matter?

Mimi For three days I haven't been able to study because of a toothache. I'm afraid of failing my final exam tomorrow.

Sam Why have you **put off** going to the dentist?

Mimi I've been hoping the pain would stop. **So far** the aspirin has been helping me sleep. But what about my final? Professor Smith will never believe my excuse.

Sam Don't worry. I'll **look after** you. I'm going to call up my dentist and tell him it's an emergency. **Get ready** and I'll drive you to his clinic?

Mimi And Professor Smith?

Sam I'll **stop by** his office tomorrow and tell him you're sick. He'll let you **put off** taking the final.

Mimi I feel better already.

IDIOM CHECK

put off /S/ Postpone; delay doing. *Don't put off till tomorrow what you can do today./ You've put off our meeting twice already. Don't put it off a third time.*

Contrast: /S/ **get (something) over with.**

so far Until now; up to this place. *So far this winter there's been lots of snow./ There's supposed to be plenty of traffic on this road, but we haven't seen one car so far.*

Equivalent: **thus far.**

look after Give care and thought to. *Would you look after my baby while I'm at the doctor's?* (Would you babysit for me?)/ *She looked after her father's store while he was away.* (She worked in the store, waited on customers, and did all the necessary things.)

Synonym: **take care of.**

get ready /S/ Prepare yourself or someone else; put yourself in a state to do something. *It's late. Get ready to leave./ The baby isn't dressed yet. Please get him ready.*

stop by Make a short and sometimes unplanned visit. *To your friend: If you have a few minutes, stop by my place this afternoon./ To someone you are visiting unexpectedly: I can stay only a minute or two. I've just stopped by to say hello./ Druggist to customer: I'll have your medicine tomorrow morning. Stop by then.*

Equivalent: **drop by, drop around.**
Compare: **stop over.**

Warning: The meaning of **stop by** depends on context. Example: *Stop by that white house. I'll get out of your car there.* (In this sentence, **by** does not belong with **stop**. Because **by** is a preposition, and a synonym of **near**, there is no idiom.)

SPELLING

put off • so far • look after • get ready • stop by
Write or say the appropriate idiom. Use one letter for each blank.

Jack has been in Dr. Brown's English class only two weeks, but _/_ _/_/_ he likes her very much. Perhaps it is because she tells funny stories. Perhaps it is because she tries to _/_/_/_ _/_/_/_/_ each student personally.

After the final bell rings, Jack _/_/_/_ _/_/_/_/_ to leave school and go home. Sometimes, however, he _/_/_/_/_ _/_ his girlfriend's house. Of course, he doesn't do his homework there. He _/_/_/_ _/_/_ doing it until he gets home.

SUBSTITUTING

Replace boldface words with appropriate idioms. Then copy or repeat aloud the whole sentence in the correct tense and person.

1. **Prepare yourself**; my boss is coming to dinner. ______________________

____.

2. Don't **delay** your dental checkup. You need it now. ______________________

____.

3. **Attend to** today and tomorrow will take care of itself. ______________________________
____.

4. **Make a short visit** to my house; I have something for you. ______________________________
____.

5. **Until now** Sam has gotten only *A's* in English. ______________________________
____.

CHOOSING

Write or say the appropriate idiom.

______________________ Mildred has *never* been late to work; she always ________ ______________ early and leaves on time. On the other hand, Bob has often been late to work; he sleeps overtime and ______________________ getting dressed until the last minute. If his wife didn't ______________________ everything, he would never get to work at all. Luckily, he has always been there the mornings that his boss __________ ____________ his office to say hello.

COMPLETING

put off • so far • look after • get ready • stop by

Give the appropriate idiom. Then finish the sentence in your own words.

1. Mimi had ______________________ her visit to the dentist until _ _ _ _ _ _
_ _.

2. ______________________ my parents have been pleased with _ _ _ _ _ _
_ _.

3. We have to ______________________ early if _ _ _ _ _ _ _ _ _ _ _ _
_ _.

4. On my way home from work yesterday, I ______________________ my aunt's house to _.

5. I want my son to stay healthy, so I ______________________ him carefully and
_ _.

CONTEXTUALIZING

In your own words, write (or tell) a story. Include all five idioms from this lesson and use the ideas below. (75 to 100 words)

1) My car has always been checked and repaired by good mechanics. 2) Today a new mechanic worked on it all day. 3) Something had gone wrong with its motor, but he didn't find what the trouble was. 4) I will probably have to delay my trip. 5) I feel so unhappy that I might visit a bar on the way home. 6) What good does it do to prepare yourself for an early start if you have a bad mechanic?

VALUING

Discuss (write about) what you think is dishonesty, using your idioms.

A. Pierre's teacher caught him cheating on his final exam and threw his exam in the wastebasket. The next day Pierre asked his teacher to retake the exam. She said, "Pierre you know the rules. Why should I make an exception for you?" When he told her that he would fail the course otherwise and she still refused, he left her office, slamming the door. Who was right in this situation? Say why.

B. Do situations like this happen in schools in your native country?

C. Can you appeal to your teacher's superiors or is his or her decision final?

D. If you do something wrong, do you often, sometimes, never get another chance?

Colorful saying: It's like pulling teeth. It's a difficult task. Often said of getting a stubborn person to do something.

Lesson 29

SAM PROPOSES

ROLE PLAYING

Sam Mimi, you've been crying!

Mimi Oh, Sam, I've lost two teeth. The dentist **took** them **out.**

Sam Do they hurt **so much**?

Mimi No, but I'll have to wear false teeth—like my father.

Sam Poor darling!

Mimi Will it **make a difference** to you? Will you still love me?

Sam Nothing can **keep** me **from** loving you, Mimi.

Mimi How can I be sure?

Sam Because—because I want to marry you.

Mimi **Never mind** being polite. You only feel sorry for me.

Sam Come here you beautiful woman.

Mimi Ohhhhhh. . . .

Sam Ahhhhhh. . . .

IDIOM CHECK

take out/S/ Remove; extract. *Sam reached in his pocket and took out a dollar bill./ Carol had a toothache, so her dentist took the tooth out.*

Contrast: **put in; put back.**

so much Considerable; a very large quantity of—**that**, stated or understood, introduces a following clause. *Jimmy has so much free time (THAT) He doesn't know what to do with it./ Parents to child: We've done so much for you (THAT) you ought to do something for us./ Jack is so much taller than Jerry (THAT) I'd never guess they're brothers.*

Synonym: **a great deal.**

make a difference Change the situation; be of importance. *Will it make a difference whether we leave Tuesday or Wednesday?/ I haven't done some of my homework. Will it make a difference in my grade?* (Will my missing homework lower my grade?)

keep from /S/ Stop yourself—or someone else—from doing something; prevent; refrain or refrain from + ING. *Mimi looked so ridiculous, Sam couldn't keep from laughING./ I grabbed the cup to keep it from breakING.*

Compare: **keep away from.**

never mind Don't trouble about it; don't worry about it; forget it—primarily used in conversation; not used in speaking to "superiors." *Never mind getting lunch ready. I'll eat in a restaurant./ Brother: Are you ready to leave? Sister: Not for twenty minutes. Brother: Then never mind. I'll go by myself.*

SPELLING

take out • so much • make a difference • keep from • never mind
Write or say the appropriate idiom. Use one letter for each blank.

Julie is rich. She has _/_ _/_/_/_ money that she can never spend it all, but she seldom _/_/_/_/_ any of it _/_/_ of the bank except for necessities.

What is important in life? Julie thinks that it is money that _/_/_/_/_ _ _/_/_/_/_/_/_/_/_/_/_. "_/_/_/_/_ _/_/_/_ about friends," she says. "Just give me money. It is money that _/_/_/_/_ _/_ _/_/_/_ being unhappy."

SUBSTITUTING

Replace boldface words with appropriate idioms. Then copy or repeat aloud the whole sentence in the correct tense and person.

1. (Who's going to pay the check?) **Don't worry about it**. I'll pay ____.

2. Larry had a bad appendix, so the doctor **removed** it. ____.

3. My homework **prevents** me **from** going to parties and dances. ____.

4. Has knowing Mimi **caused changes** in Sam's life? ____.

5. My mother worried **such a lot** that she became ill. ____.

CHOOSING

Write or say the appropriate idiom.

Last week Mimi ____________ all her clothes ____________ the closet and pressed them. She felt it was important to look neat; being well dressed ____________ to her.

Of course, Mimi always liked buying clothes— ____________ the cost! Nothing gave her ____________ happiness. A new skirt or dress always ____________ feeling sad and stopped her from worrying.

COMPLETING

take out • so much • make a difference • keep from • never mind

Give the appropriate idiom. Then finish the sentence in your own words.

1. Charles had drunk ____________ whiskey that _ .
2. The doctor had ____________ her left eye because _ .
3. My father is feeling better. The new medicine has ____________ in _ .
4. ____________ phoning for a taxi. Bob isn't going to _ .
5. Being poor has ____________ me ____________ being _ .

CONTEXTUALIZING

In your own words, write (or tell) a story. Include all five idioms from this lesson and use the ideas below. (75 to 100 words)

1) Bill was divorced. 2) But being single again was no fun. 3) He liked to have female friends. 4) To make himself attractive, he bought nice clothes. 5) He spent all his savings. 6) He couldn't stop himself. 7) Don't worry about Bill—he'll find a rich wife. 8) Then he'll spend her money.

VALUING

Discuss (write about) the situation below, using your idioms.

A. To Mary's family, Bill would be the perfect husband for her: 28 years old, rich, of the same religion as Mary, he is liked by everybody. Mary has known and dated him for several months, but she isn't sure she wants to marry him. Mary's father has reminded her that there is more to marriage than romantic love. Being in poor health, he would feel better knowing that Mary has a good husband and a secure future. She wants to please him, and marriage with Bill would not make her unhappy. However, she feels that love is important and that there is more to life than security. Imagine you are Mary's brother or sister. What will you tell her to do? Why?

B. In your country, are marriages always, sometimes, or never arranged?

C. What would be the advantages or disadvantages of an arranged marriage?

Colorful saying: Have a screw loose. Act strangely or foolishly.

Lesson 30

CALLING UP SAM'S PARENTS

ROLE PLAYING

Mimi **Take it easy**, darling. Your parents will be glad when you phone them and say we're getting married.

Sam No, they won't. Even today many Japanese marriages are **more or less** arranged. When my father hears that I'm marrying a girl he's never met . . . wow!

Mimi *Wow?*

Sam He's **short of** patience. He might not listen.

Mimi Won't I **get to** speak to him?

Sam The problem is—will *I* **get to** speak to him?

Mimi Sam, your father may be **short of** patience, but—believe me—I'm **out of** patience. If you want to marry me, phone *now.*

IDIOM CHECK

take it easy Relax (mentally and/or physically); avoid work and worry. *After his heart attack, my boss had to take it easy./ Take it easy! Our professor never gives hard tests.*

Equivalent: **take things easy.**

more or less To an undetermined degree; somewhat. *My 6-year-old son more or less believes in Santa Claus.*

Contrast: **not at all.**

be short of Not having enough. *Quick! Find my car keys. I'm short of time!/ Could you lend me $5? I'm short of cash.*

Compare: **run short of.**

get to + base form of verb Have the chance to; be able to; succeed in. *It rained, so we didn't get to play baseball./ Friend: Have you gotten to see Professor Smith? You told me he has a busy schedule. You: Yes, I got to see him yesterday.*

be out of Having none left; be without. *I ran up the stairs. Now I'm out of breath./ The car is out of gas. That's why it won't start.*

Compare: **run out of.**
Contrast: **have plenty of.**

SPELLING

take it easy • more or less • be short of • get to • be out of
Write or say the appropriate idiom. Use one letter for each blank.

Suzy is _/_/_/_ _/_ _/_/_/_ timid. She likes boys, but every time she _/_/_/_ _/_ date one, she doesn't know what to say to him. She finds herself _/_/_/_/_ _/_ ideas. Instead of relaxing and _/_/_/_/_/_ _/_ _/_/_/_ , she becomes very nervous, has difficulty breathing, and ends the evening _/_/_ _/_ breath and ready to cry.

SUBSTITUTING

Replace boldface words with appropriate idioms. Then copy or repeat aloud the whole sentence in the correct tense and person.

1. I can't cook a cake. I **have no** flour. ____________________________ .

2. I can't lend you $100. I **don't have enough** money. ________________________ .

3. **Relax**! You are sure to win. ____________________________ .

4. Have you **had the chance to** go to Canada? ____________________________ .

5. We were **somewhat** surprised to hear of Mimi's engagement. ________________________ .

CHOOSING

Write or say the appropriate idiom.

Mimi first ____________ know Sam at school. Between classes they would relax, talk together, and ____________. They soon began to date, but they could only go to cheap movies because Sam was ____________ broke. He had just enough money to pay for his board and room, so he was always ____________ cash. For any evening that cost more than $10, Mimi was ____________ luck.

COMPLETING

take it easy • more or less • be short of • get to • be out of
Give the appropriate idiom. Then finish the sentence in your own words.

1. ____________! Don't get upset. It isn't _ .

2. The only thing worse than being completely ____________ money is _ .

3. When Senator Kennedy visited your college, did you ____________ talk to him and _ _ _ _ _ _ _ _ _ _ _ _ _ _ _ _ _ _ _ ?

4. I was ____________ tired after _ .

5. Maria was ____________ time, so _ .

CONTEXTUALIZING

In your own words, write (or tell) a story. Include all five idioms from this lesson and use the ideas below. (75 to 100 words)

1) Tom is very friendly. 2) He kisses lots of girls. 3) He loves—somewhat—every girl he kisses. 4) But girls don't love Tom. 5) They don't have much patience with him. 6) He has no luck. 7) He has bad breath. 8) If only he would stop kissing girls, they would like him better.

VALUING

Discuss (write about) marriage, using your idioms.

A. Time: 1991. Married and living with Sam in Tokyo, Mimi has just asked him for a divorce. He has agreed. Can you imagine what went wrong with their marriage? (Think about differences in their character and background.)

B. In your native country what do people consider to be the advantages of marriage? Its disadvantages? For men? For women?

C. In the United States one marriage in two ends in divorce. Can you suggest why this happens? Too easy divorce? Too early marriage (both partners too young)? Not enough money? A lack of a sense of family? Women's liberation? Unrealistic expectations (romantic, sexual)?

Colorful saying: "A man is incomplete until he is married. After that, he is finished." (Zsa Zsa Gabor)

Idiom Review of Lessons 28, 29, 30

Directions

a. Add letters to each circle so as to make an idiom.

b. Find the definition below that fits each idiom and put its *number* in the small circle.

c. Add the numbers in the circles across (⟶) or down (↓). The numbers *must* total 34. To help you start, one circle is already done.

Definitions

1. give care and thought to
2. cause changes
3. relax
4. have the chance to
5. somewhat; to some extent
6. until now
7. manage without; omit
8. remove; extract
9. not to concern or bother yourself
10. a very large quantity; to a great degree
11. not having enough
12. delay; postpone
13. having none left
14. visit
15. prepare yourself
16. stop yourself from doing something; restrain yourself

YOU HAVEN'T HEARD THE LAST OF IT

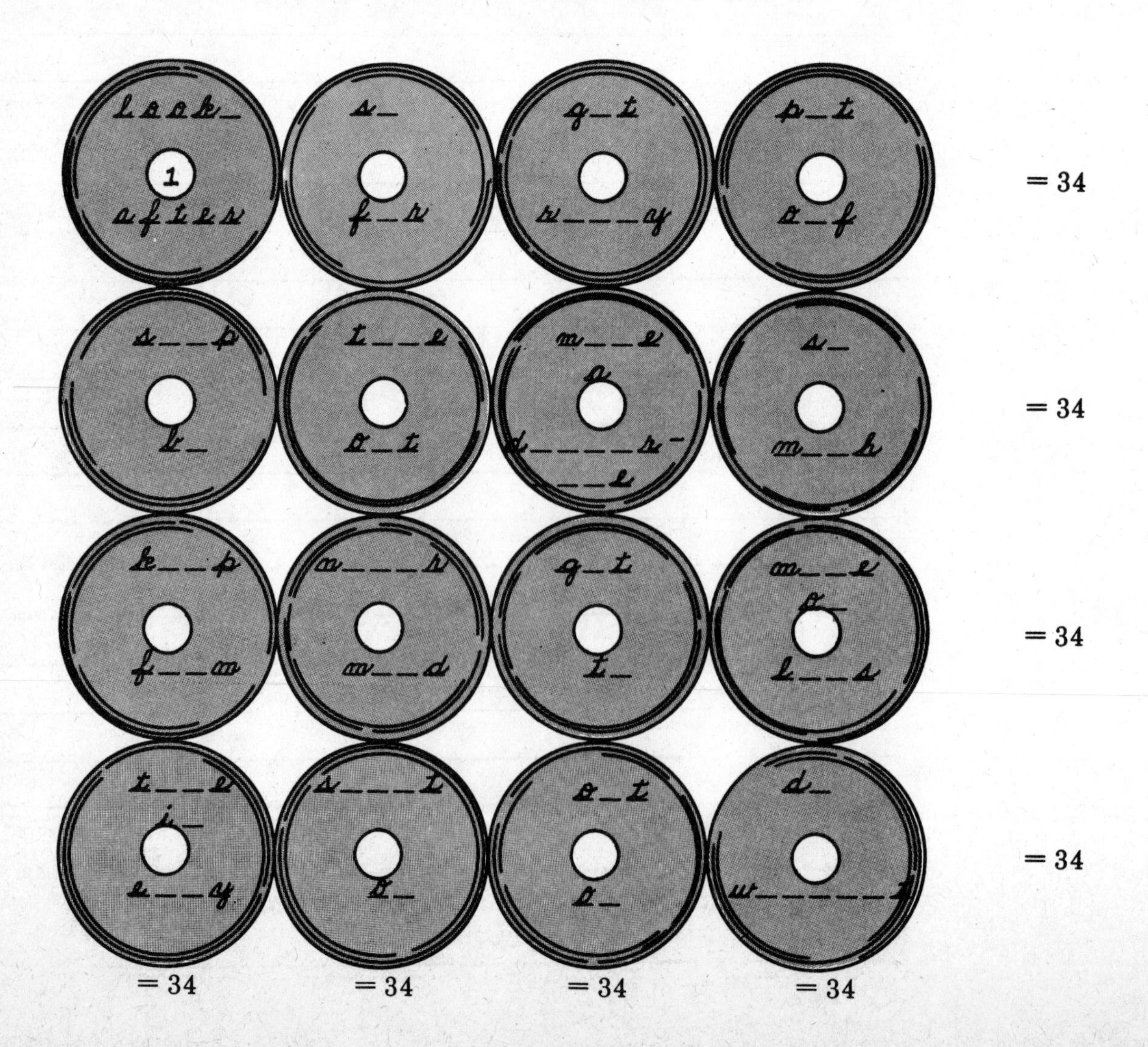

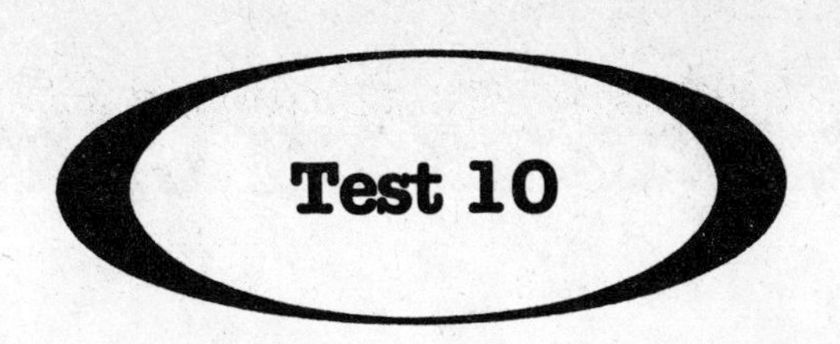

Test 10

Level I. From the **Completing** exercise of lessons 28, 29, 30, your teacher will choose five incomplete sentences and read them to you. Write them down, supply appropriate idioms for them, and finish them in your own words.

1 ____________________

2 ____________________

3 ____________________

4 ____________________

5 ____________________

Level II. The pictures tell a story. In one paragraph of 120 to 150 words, tell this story or write it on a separate piece of paper. Include any five of these idioms: **look after / get ready / make a difference / get to / more or less**

CONTRACTIONS BY CATEGORY

I Personal Pronoun + Auxiliary Verb

I'm	I am	I've	I have
you're	you are	you've	you have
he's	he is	he's	he has
she's	she is	she's	she has
it's	it is	it's	it has
we're	we are	we've	we have
they're	they are	they've	they have
I'll	I will	I'd	I had, I would
you'll	you will	you'd	you had, you would
he'll	he will	he'd	he had, he would
she'll	she will	she'd	she had, she would
it'll	it will	it'd	it had, it would
we'll	we will	we'd	we had, we would
they'll	they will	they'd	they had, they would

II Relative Pronoun + Auxiliary Verb

that's	that is	that'll	that will
what's	what is	what'll	what will
who's	who is	who'll	who will
		who'd	who had, who would

III Auxiliary Verb + Not

isn't	is not	won't	will not
aren't	are not	wouldn't	would not
wasn't	was not	shouldn't	should not
weren't	were not	can't	cannot
haven't	have not	couldn't	could not
hasn't	has not	mightn't	might not
hadn't	had not	oughtn't	ought not
		mustn't	must not
don't	do not		
doesn't	does not		
didn't	did not		

IV Adverb + Auxiliary Verb

how's	how is
when's	when is
where's	where is

V Expletives

here's	here is
there's	there is

TO THE STUDENT

If you want your speech to sound natural, not stiff, use these contracted forms.

COMMON ELLIPTICAL CONSTRUCTIONS*

Definition: *Ellipsis* means omitting the word or words necessary to make the sentence(s) complete. The context tells you what is missing.

I. *Examples of three kinds of ellipsis* (Refer to Dialog 2 in this book.):

1. **Repetition:** One person agrees or disagrees with what the other says and *repeats* it.
   Mimi Are you prejudiced against France?
   Sam *I'm not* (prejudiced against France).

2. **Expansion:** One person agrees or disagrees with what the other says and *adds* to it. The answer is *more than* a simple yes or no.
   Mimi Are you calling me prejudiced?
   Sam *Maybe* (I am calling you prejudiced).

3. **Replacement:** One person agrees or disagrees with what the other says and *replaces* it *with new material.*
   Mimi Someone that you met in Japan?
   Sam *No,* (it was someone that I met) *here in San Francisco.*

II. A. *In a series of sentences, once you say the subject and the verb, you can omit one or both.*

B. *In place of an idea developed by one or more sentences, you can substitute a word such as SO, THAT, or THIS.*
   Sam People are different. French, Japanese, Americans—they're all different.
   A
   (They are) *Not superior or inferior.*
   A *B*
   (They are) *Different.* You ought to know *this.* (*This* = idea developed by the preceding sentences.)

III. *You can use ellipsis without having a verbal context.*
   Sam (Are you) *Trying to find someone?* (A first line: no verbal context yet exists.)

In everyday speech (greetings, apologies, offers of help, etc.), you will often hear this kind of ellipsis:
   (It's) *Good to see you.*
   (I am) *Sorry I couldn't be there.*
   (Does) *Anybody need a ride?*

*The above material has been adapted and paraphrased from Randolph Quirk and Sidney Greenbaum, *A Concise Grammar of Contemporary English,* Harcourt Brace Jovanovich, Inc., New York, 1973. See pp. 253, 305–308.

NAMES AND NICKNAMES

A nickname is a name your friends call you, not your legal name. Note that many nicknames end in *y* or *ie*.

Given Name (male)	Nickname	Given Name (female)	Nickname
Andrew	Andy	Amy	—
Benjamin	Ben	Angela	Angie
Charles	Chuck, Charlie	Ann(e)	Annie
Christopher	Chris	Barbara	Barb
David	Dave	Betty	Bet
Donald	Don	Carol	—
Edward	Ed, Ted(dy)	Christine	Chris
Frank	—	Doris	—
Frederick	Fred	Dorothy	Dottie
George	—	Elizabeth	Liz, Beth
Gerald	Jerry	Emily	—
Henry	Hank, Harry	Frances	Fran(ny)
Herbert	Herb	Geraldine	Gerry
James	Jim, Jimmy	Helen	—
Jeffrey	Jeff	Jane	—
John	Jack, Johnny	Jean	Jeanie
Joseph	Joe	Joan	Joanie
Lawrence	Larry	K(C)atherine	Kate, Cathy
Michael	Mike	Kimberly	Kim
Patrick	Pat	Linda	—
Peter	Pete	Margaret	Marge, Peggy
Raymond	Ray	Mary	—
Richard	Dick, Rich	Mildred	Millie
Robert	Bob, Bobby, Rob	Nancy	—
Samuel	Sam, Sammy	Patricia	Pat(ty)
Stephen	Steve	Ruth	—
Thomas	Tom, Tommy	Sally	—
Timothy	Tim, Timmy	Sarah	—
William	Bill, Billy	Susan	Sue, Suzy
		Virginia	Ginnie

LEXICON

A

about time 13 something that should have happened earlier. After knowing her for ten years, it's *about time* he married her.

about to 20 ready to; on the point of. Hurry! The bus is *about to* leave.

ahead of time SL* early. My appointment was at three o'clock, but the doctor told me I could come *ahead of time.*

all along 22 from the beginning; always. I wasn't surprised when the police arrested John. I knew *all along* that he was dishonest.

all at once 18 suddenly; unexpectedly; without warning. *All at once* I heard an explosion and every window in my house broke.

all day long 12 the whole day. I felt ill yesterday, so I stayed in bed *all day long.*

all in all 21 everything considered; everything counted; in summary. A few things went wrong, but *all in all* we had a pleasant day. Two oranges and two apples: *all in all,* that makes four pieces of fruit.

all right 11 a) okay; satisfactory.** Is it *all right* if Jane comes with us? b) unhurt; well. Are you *all right* now? You won't be sick again?

all the time 13 a) continually. Betty talks *all the time.* Nobody else can say a word. b) during a particular period of time. I looked everywhere for my key and it was in my pocket *all the time.*

as for 10 with reference to; concerning. Bob wants to play golf. *As for me,* I want to go swimming.

ask for /S/* 20** a) request something; ask to be given something. Nancy was thirsty, so she *asked for* a glass of water. b) risk something unpleasant happening. Ray drives too fast. He is *asking for* an accident.

as usual 15 as is or was the custom; most of the time. *As usual,* Emily was late for class.

as yet 21 until now; up to the present. *As yet,* I don't earn much money.

at all see **not at all 11**

at first SL at the beginning. *At first,* I hated American food. However, I soon learned to like it.

at home 3 in one's house. Phone me tonight. I'll be *at home.*

at last 26 after a long time; finally. My sister was returning to America after ten years absence. *At last* I was going to see her again.

at (the) least 15 not less than. They need *at least* three hours to finish their work.

at (the) most 7 not more than; maximum. We can give you five dollars *at the most.* Don't ask for more.

at the same time 4 a) happening in the same moment or period of time. Mimi and Sam finished the test *at the same time*—exactly noon. b) but; however; nevertheless. Mary can be very kind; *at the same time,* she can be the worst person I know.

*SL = sample lesson

**Although the same idiom may have different meanings (a, b, c, etc.), it will have only meaning (a) in the lesson.

***/S/ indicates a separable idiom. A noun or pronoun may be inserted between its words.

Example: **ask for /S/** She *asked* Bill *for* a drink.
She *asked* him *for* a drink.

B

be broke **4** have no money—usually a temporary condition. *I'm broke* today. Can you lend me a dollar?

be out of **30** having none left; be without. I hope you like beer. We'*re out of* wine.

be short of **30** not having enough. John never waits for anyone; he'*s short of* patience.

be used to **5** be accustomed to. Eskimos *are used to* snow and ice.

bring up /S/ **9** a) raise (a subject or question); introduce a subject into discussion. Mary's father died last week. Don't *bring up* his name when you meet her. b) care for in childhood; rear. My mother *brought up* seven children.

by far **16** greatly; obviously; by a great margin. Mary is *by far* the prettiest girl in our class.

by the way **17** incidentally; in that connection (but of secondary interest). I don't intend to invite Bill to my party. *By the way,* he won't be surprised. He knows I don't like him.

C

call off /S/ **23** cancel; decide against doing, having, etc. It was raining, so our coach *called off* the baseball game.

call on **12** a) visit. Every time I go to Philadelphia, I *call on* my sister. b) ask to participate or contribute. My professor is always *calling on* me in class.

call up /S/ **22** a) telephone. I'll *call* you *up* tomorrow at nine. b) bring to mind. The old film *called up* my boyhood memories.

catch cold **8** become ill with a cold. When I drive my car with its windows open, I *catch cold.*

change (one's) mind **2** alter one's decision. We *changed our mind.* We're not going to Europe next summer.

come back **1** a) return to the same place where you now are; return *here.* When did you *come back* from Paris? (Same meaning: **get back**) b) return to your memory. Now I remember what happened. It's *coming back* to me now. c) become popular again. Do you think the mini skirt will *come back*?

come from **2** a) be a native of. My classmates *come from* twelve different countries. b) derive from; originate in. Many English words *come from* Latin.

come to **20** a) learn to; grow to; acquire enough familiarity or understanding to do something. I didn't like Carol when I first met her, but I *came to* love her. b) amount to. Your rent *comes to* $200 a month. c) result in. John and Mary are separated, but I hope it won't *come to* divorce. d) regain consciousness. The last thing I remembered was a car hitting me. I *came to* in the hospital.

cut down on **27** reduce, lessen. You must *cut down on* your expenses if you want to save money.

cut out /S/ **27** a) suppress; stop. The best way to lose weight is to *cut out* eating candy. *Cut out* the noise! I'm trying to study. b) remove by cutting around; excise. The boy *cut out* the pictures from the magazine.

D

do with **27** a) profit from; use with advantage. I'm cold. I could *do with* a hot cup of coffee. b) manage with (for lack of something better). Since Alice doesn't own an overcoat, she must *do with* a sweater in winter. c) be acquainted with; associate with (with *have*). Don't have anything to *do with* her. She will make you unhappy.

do without **11** manage without; live without something. In the United States, people cannot *do without* a car. Distances are too great.

E

even so **21** however; regardless; nevertheless. Al buys his wife everything she wants. *Even so,* she isn't happy. (same meaning: **just the same**)

every other **24** every second one; alternate. In summer I take a bath every day, but in winter *every other* day is enough.

F

feel up to **27** be able to; feel capable of. I slept so well that I *feel up to* playing tennis before breakfast.

figure out /S/ **16** a) understand; discover by reason. I can't *figure out* why Bob quit his job. I thought he liked it. b) calculate; solve. Do you *figure out* your income tax every year?

find fault with **8** criticize; complain about, be dissatisfied with. My boss doesn't like me, so he always tries to *find fault with* my work.

find out /S/ **9** a) learn; discover. How did you *find out* that he wasn't telling the truth? b) inquire; ask. Will you *find out* Mimi's address for me?

for once **25** this one time. *For once,* I was able to do what I always wanted; I spent the whole month swimming.

for the time being **12** temporarily; for the present moment. You can live with us *for the time being,* but you must find your own apartment soon.

from now on **1** starting now and continuing into the future; from this time forward. For months our class started at 8:00 a.m. *From now on* it will start at 9:00 a.m.

G

get along (with) **26** a) be friendly with; agree on most things. My father and I *get along* well together. We are always nice to one another. b) make progress. How are you *getting along* with your term paper? Is it almost finished? c) leave; go. I must be *getting along* now. It's late. d) manage. Jim is an excellent cook. He can *get along* quite well when his wife is away.

get behind **4** a) do something too slowly; go too slowly. Don't *get behind* in your car payments. The bank could take your car from you. b) help; support. Americans ought to *get behind* their president and help him to conserve energy.

get off **3** a) descend from; leave (a bus, train, plane, boat). We *got off* the bus at Fifth Avenue. b) remove from /S/. The ring was too tight. Doris couldn't *get* it *off* her finger.

get on **3** a) go into; enter (a bus, train, plane, boat). Jill *got on* the plane and flew to Chicago. b) live or work in friendship with someone. Jim and his brother never fight. They *get on* well together.

get on (one's) nerves **SL** irritate; bother; upset. That noise *gets on my nerves.*

get ready /S/ **28** a) prepare yourself. Can you *get ready* to leave by 6:00 p.m.? b) prepare something /S/. Could you *get* the dinner *ready* early tonight?

get rid of **2** discard; eliminate; throw away. If I had more money, I would *get rid of* my old car and buy a new one.

get the best of see **get the better of** **18**

get the better of **18** win against; beat; defeat. Bob always *gets the better of* me at chess. I can't win against him.

get to **30** a) succeed in. Freddy finally *got to* enter college and his mother was pleased. b) arrive. The train *gets to* New York at noon.

get up /S/ **SL** a) leave your bed; arise. I *get up* every morning at seven. b) stand up; get to your feet. On a bus Henry always *gets up* and gives a woman his seat.

give back /S/ **24** return. *Give* me *back* my book. I need it for my homework.

give up /S/ **9** a) abandon; stop/renounce. Smoking is bad for your health. You ought to *give* it *up*. b) surrender. When the robbers realized they couldn't escape, they *gave up*. c) (for persons and things) abandon. I *gave* her *up* for dead. She wasn't breathing.

go ahead **25** begin immediately; start to do something without waiting. *Go ahead* and eat. Don't let your food get cold.

go away **22** depart; leave. My brother *goes away* to school this fall.

go back **1** a) return to a different place than where you presently are; return *there*. Maria was originally from Mexico; she wants to *go back* and visit her parents. b) revert. Sam *went back* to his old habits. He's smoking again. c) date back. My family *goes back* to the American Revolution. d) extend back in space. My garden *goes back* to the red wall.

go on **2** a) happen. I wonder what is *going on* in the United States. I haven't read our newspaper for a week. b) continue. It's early. We can *go on* playing football for another hour. c) continue talking. She *went on* about her troubles for an hour.

go too far **11** pass beyond a reasonable limit. Bill *goes too far* when he lies to his own mother.

go up **18** a) rise; increase. Food prices have been *going up* for two years now. b) ascent; mount. If you *go up* those stairs, be careful. The third step is broken. c) be built. New buildings are *going up* everywhere.

H

had better **6** ought to; would be wise to. If you want to pass that exam, you *had better* study.

have a good time **7** enjoy oneself. I *had a good time* at your party. I danced the whole evening.

have (someone) do (something) **25** make somebody do something, cause him to do it. My mother *has* me *finish* my *homework* before I watch TV.

have in mind **23** intend; plan. I *had in mind* going to a play tonight. O.K.?

have on /S/ **26** a) be wearing. Did Beth *have* her hat *on* last night? b) have something arranged; have plans for. I *have* nothing *on* this week. Visit me whenever you want.

have over /S/ **11** invite. We would like to *have* you *over* for dinner next week. (In British usage: have in.)

have (got) to **3** must; ought to. Every day I *have to* be at the office at nine sharp.

hear from **15** a) receive a letter, phone call, news, etc., from someone. Did you *hear from* your parents lately? b) receive information from somebody /S/. I *heard* it *from* Henry. Our teacher is getting married.

How come? **9** How is it possible? Explain what you mean. You say John is sick! *How come?* I just met him in the street.

I

in a hurry **10** rushed; with a need to move or act quickly. Bill's *in a hurry*. His plane leaves in ten minutes.

in a while **13** later; at some time in the future. Son: Dad, will you help me with my homework? Father: *In a while*. I'm listening to the news now.

in fact **5** really; indeed; in reality. George is very religious. *In fact*, he wants to become a priest.

instead of **26** in place of; rather than. When I went in his room, my brother was sleeping *instead of* studying.

in time **6** a) early enough. I rarely come home *in time* to watch the six o'clock news. b) eventually. *In time* you will learn to like American food.

it's a question of **19** it concerns. We cannot go to Europe this summer. *It's* not *a question of* money; *it's a question of* time.

it's no wonder see **no wonder** **7**

J

just now **25** a minute ago; this very moment. You can still catch Jane on the stairs. She left *just now.*

K

keep from /S/ **29** a) restrain or refrain from. Bill looked so funny that I couldn't *keep from* laughing. b) prevent. As it fell, I grabbed the glass and *kept* it *from* breaking.

keep on + ING **16** continue. Dan is stupid. He *keeps on* making the same mistakes. The rain *kept on* falling for seven days.

keep quiet /S/ *23* a) remain silent. *Keep quiet* and listen to me. b) stop (someone or something) from talking or making noise. *Keep* (him) *quiet* while I'm studying.

keep up with **14** a) be aware of. I try to *keep up with* what's happening in the world. b) go or move as fast as (of motion). Mike walks so fast his wife can't *keep up with* him. c) maintain the pace; stay even with (of any activity). John can't *keep up with* the rest of the class; he's going to fail math.

L

leave out /S/ **16** a) omit. When Mary told the story, she *left out* some important facts. b) leave available. If I come home late, my wife always *leaves out* some food for me.

let (somebody) alone **19** allow somebody to be undisturbed. *Let* me *alone.* I have to study for my test.

let (somebody) know **27** inform; tell. *Let* me *know* when you are ready and we shall go.

let (me, us) see **17** allow me to think; to consider. (Hello! I would like to make an appointment with the dentist.) Well, *let me see.* Can you come tomorrow at 2:00 p.m.?

let go of **24** release. Don't *let go of* the bottle or it will fall.

look after **28** a) watch over; attend to; give care and thought to. My mother *looks after* my children while I'm at work. b) attend to temporarily. Will you *look after* my house plants while I'm on vacation?

look for /S/ **24** search for; seek. Would you help me *look for* my keys? I think I've lost them.

look forward to + ING **15** anticipate with pleasure. I'm *looking forward to* going to Japan. I *look forward to* your visit next month.

look into **16** investigate; examine. The police *looked into* the robbery.

look up /S/ **23** a) research; search in a book. Wait a minute! Let me *look up* the exact address in the phone book. I *looked* it *up* for you. b) improve; prosper. Business is *looking up* again. I sold three cars last week. c) visit. I'm going to Boston next week. I think I'll *look up* John.

M

make a difference **29** a) change the situation; cause a change. The death of my father *made a* big *difference* in my life. b) matter; be of importance. It doesn't *make a difference* to me whether you come tonight or not.

make a living **12** earn enough to live adequately. He works days and nights to *make a living.*

make a point of **14** insist upon; give importance to. My mother *makes a point of* remembering my birthday.

make fun of **22** laugh at; ridicule. When Helene speaks English, her friends *make fun of* her accent.

make out /S/ **24** a) understand; interpret. Can you *make out* why she behaves so rudely? b) identify; distinguish. It's too dark. I can't *make out* the street numbers. c) complete or fill in. Mimi *made out* a check for $100. I *made out* an application blank for the job. d) do; succeed. Sam *makes out* very well in Mrs. Smith's class. He always gets A's.

make sense **10** be intelligible; be reasonable. Henry tells us that he is poor. It doesn't *make sense* because I know he makes $25,000 a year.

make sure **15** be certain, cause to be certain. I *made sure* the door was locked before I left.

may as well see **might as well 20**

might as well **20** could do with equal or better effect; is somewhat preferable. I have finished my work. I *might as well* go home now.

more or less **30** somewhat; to some extent. Bob drinks too much. He is *more or less* drunk every time I see him.

N

never mind **29** forget it; don't trouble about it. Don't worry about it. When I asked her what she said, she told me: "*Never mind.* It wasn't important."

no matter **19** regardless of. *No matter* how well I do my work, my boss always finds something wrong.

not at all **11** not in the least; not even in the smallest amount. It was December, but the weather was *not at all* cold.

not much of a **19** rather bad. A noisy motel is *not much of a* place to sleep.

no wonder **7** naturally; it is not surprising. (It's) *no wonder* he didn't arrive! His airplane crashed.

O

of course **SL** naturally. Are you coming to our party? *Of course*, I am. I love parties.

once and for all **21** finally; permanently; conclusively. *Once and for all* do what I tell you! I won't say it again.

once in a while **13** occasionally. Our son comes to see us *once in a while*, mainly when he needs money.

on purpose **22** intentionally; for a reason. She broke that glass *on purpose.* She was really angry.

on the other hand **9** from the opposite point of view. I like winters in Florida; *on the other hand,* I prefer the cool summers of Maine.

on the whole **5** a) in general. *On the whole,* Americans are nice people. b) all things considered. Sam doesn't always attend class, but *on the whole* he is a good student.

on time **6** punctually; exactly at a fixed time. Our train is rarely *on time*; it can be as much as 15 minutes late.

P

pick out /S/ **7** a) select; choose. *Pick out* the ring you like and I'll buy it for you. b) recognize. I can't always *pick out* my friends in a large crowd.

pick up /S/ **18** a) involving lifting and actions related to it concretely and abstractly: lift, obtain, gather acquire. After he fell, Sam *picked* himself *up*. The driver *picked up* the hitchhiker. She *picked up* the book and read it. I'll *pick up* a new necktie at the department store. b) correct; reprimand. Mimi made a mistake in English and Professor Smith *picked* her *up* on it. c) become casually acquainted with. Bill had never met Mary before; he *picked* her *up* at a dance. d) arrest; catch. The police *picked up* the robber at the airport.

point out /S/ **17** a) mention; explain. He *pointed out* that I would fail English if I didn't study. b) show. *Point out* the Student Center to me, please.

put in /S/ **10** a) to spend time in a specified manner. It's a shame Jeff failed his exam. He *put in* a whole week studying for it. b) insert. If you write to Jane, *put in* a few words about my trip.

put off /S/ **28** a) postpone; delay. You complain about your health, but you always *put off* going to the doctor. b) evade answering questions or giving information. Each time I ask for my money back, Jack *puts* me *off.* c) discourage. The professor *put* me *off* by his angry words. I wanted to quit the course.

put on /S/ **8** a) dress in; clothe oneself. Shall I *put on* a long dress for the party? b) add. Last year Matthew *put on* ten pounds. Now he looks fat. c) fool; kid (slang). You're *putting* me *on*, aren't you? It's not true that you're quitting your job?

put up with **14** tolerate. George *put up with* his wife's bad temper for years, but finally he divorced her.

Q

quite a few **6** more than a few; a lot of. This restaurant must be good; there are *quite a few* people in it.

R

read up on **23** study by reading about. I'm *reading up on* American history because I have an exam tomorrow.

right away **5** immediately. Please wait a minute. Anita said that she would come back *right away.*

run into **3** a) meet by chance. Yesterday I *ran into* an old friend on the street. What a pleasant surprise to see him again! b) crash into; collide with. He *ran into* me with his car and broke my legs. c) encounter. He *ran into* trouble in his English course. d) add up to. It *runs into* a lot of money. Can you pay it?

run out of **24** a) come to the end of; exhaust a supply of something. My car *ran out of* gas on the highway. b) force to leave /S/. My landlady *ran* me *out of* my room because I didn't pay my rent.

S

see to **1** a) give attention to; undertake. While my boyfriend *saw to* parking his car, I bought the movie tickets. (same meaning: **see about**) b) fix; repair. Your socks have holes in them. They need *seeing to.*

so far **28** until now. *So far* we are quite satisfied with the car we bought last month.

so much **29** a) adj. considerable; a very large quantity of. I have *so much* work that I won't be able to finish before supper. b) adv. considerably; to such a degree. I studied *so much* that I'm very tired.

sooner or later **12** inevitably; ultimately; eventually. You'll have to study *sooner or later.* Why not now?

step by step **21** gradually; by degrees. *Step by step* the boy learned to read.

stop by **28** visit; pass by. On our way home, we *stopped by* Jim's house for a few minutes. We'll *stop by* at seven o'clock and take you to the play.

T

take advantage of **7** a) profit from; make use of. We *took advantage of* our trip to Japan to buy a new camera. b) gain at the expense of another; use unfairly. The salesman *took advantage of* my ignorance to sell me a bad TV set.

take a trip **4** go for a journey. Every summer I *take a trip* to Europe.

take it easy **30** relax. *Take it easy!* The dentist said it wouldn't hurt you. I've been working for several weekends. This weekend I'm going to *take it easy.*

take off **8** a) remove (usually one's clothes). You can't wear that ridiculous dress to the opera. *Take* it *off* and wear something more conservative. b) (of aircraft) leave the ground and rise. Fasten your seatbelt. Our plane is *taking off.* c) be absent from work. I felt sick, so I *took* the day *off* from work. d) deduct. The car had a dent in the front door so the dealer *took* $10 *off* its price.

take out /S/ **29** a) remove; extract. He *took out* his wallet and gave me the money. b) accompany; escort. Sorry, I cannot go with you tonight. Henry *takes* me *out* every Saturday. c) acquire. Juan *took out* an automobile insurance policy.

take part in **17** participate. Today, I *took part in* a class discussion on abortion.

take place **20** happen; occur. We told Fanny what *took place* in her absence. She was shocked.

take up /S/ **18** a) undertake; begin; adopt. On his doctor's recommendation, Harry *took up* golf as an exercise. b) occupy space or time. That bed *takes up* too much space in my room. c) return to. Sam *took up* his story where Mimi had interrupted him. d) shorten. Mimi *took up* all her skirts.

talk (something) over **6** discuss. Fanny and Sam *talked over* their vacation plans.

tell A from B **19** distinguish between. Barbara and Betty are twins. When I meet them, I can never *tell* Barbara *from* Betty.

that is **17** to say it more exactly. I wish I could speak English, *that is*, speak it well.

think of **5** a) have an opinion. What do you *think of* my new dress? b) consider; intend to. We are *thinking of* buying a new house. c) give attention to. My son has his future to *think of*. He must do his schoolwork.

think (something) over **8** consider carefully before deciding. Don't decide now. *Think* it *over* for a few days, and then give me your answer.

time off **4** time for oneself; a period of release from work. I took *time off* from studying and went to a movie.

turn off /S/ **14** shut off; close; stop. Don't leave the water running. *Turn* it *off*, please. Please *turn off* the lights before you leave the room.

turn on /S/ **14** let come; let flow; open. It's getting dark. *Turn* the lights *on*, please.

U

used to **13** a) had the habit of. I *used to* smoke three packages of cigarettes a day. b) formerly did—a state or condition. We *used to* live in New York.

W

What about. . . ? **10** a) How would you like. . . ? It has been a hot day. *What about* a cool drink? b) request for information. My mother has recovered from her accident. *What about* your father?

what's more **2** furthermore; besides; in addition. My boss gave me a twenty-dollar raise. *What's more,* he offered me my own office.

What's the matter? **1** What's happening? What's wrong? *What's the matter?* You look very pale suddenly!

would rather **26** prefer. *I'd rather* see a movie than study tonight. I *would rather* live than die.

STUDENT'S LOG[1]

(When you or somebody else **used**[2] an **idiom**[3] outside class)

NAME ______________________________

Idiom used	How the idiom was used[4]	Persons involved	Purpose (or reason)	Topic (or event)	Place	What were the circumstances? Why did using the idiom seem to succeed or fail?	Day and time
take it easy	face-to-face	A teacher and me	I wanted to apologize	My knocking into her	On the stairs of the school	I told her to *take it easy* because she seemed angry at me and I wanted her to relax. Then she told me I was impolite. Can't I use this idiom with teachers?	April 3 2 p.m.

[1]Log = record
[2]Used = spoken, heard, read, or written.
[3]Idiom = any idiom, in your book or not.
[4]How used = face-to-face, overheard, on the phone, in writing, on TV, on radio, in a magazine, etc.

INDEX*

*Numbers 1–30 = Lessons 1–30. SL = Sample Lesson.

†/S/ after an idiom means that an American or English speaker often *separates* it by inserting a noun or a pronoun between its words.

Example: **ask for** /S/ She *asked for* a drink.
She *asked* Bill *for* a drink.
She *asked* him *for* a drink.

CORRECTION GUIDE

To the student: The numbers below indicate different kinds of idiom mistakes. Your teacher will write these numbers above your mistakes to help you make corrections.

1 Verb form (of the idiom)

I am thinking of Sam as a good man.
I think of Sam as a good man.

Explanation: Verbal idioms of knowing, perceiving, or having personal attitudes cannot take the continuous.

2 Verb form (of verbs going before or after the idiom)

a. We learned a lot up to now.
We have learned a lot up to now.

Explanation: Some adverbial idioms require the verb they modify to take a certain tense.

b. Mimi gave up to try to pass the test.
Mimi gave up trying to pass the test.

Explanation: Verbal idioms followed by another verb require that verb to be a gerund.

3 Word order

I wanted to learn tennis, so I took up it.
I wanted to learn tennis, so I took it up.

Explanation: Separable verbal idioms (p. 39) require a certain word order.

4 Overgeneralization

She got on the automobile.
She got into the automobile.

Explanation: *Get on* can be used with planes, trains, boats and bicycles, but its meaning doesn't include automobiles.

5 Non-idiomatic

Maria ran into the school where she met John.
Maria ran into John at school.

Explanation: The sentence is correct, but because *run into* is part of your idiom lesson, you must use it there as an idiom meaning *meet someone.*

6 Illogical

a. Ali liked Sue. On the other hand, he liked her sister.
Ali liked Sue. On the other hand, he disliked her sister.

Explanation: The student misunderstands this "transitional" idiom and, therefore, illogically connects two sentences.

b. As for me, you need to see a doctor.
As for you, you need to see a doctor.

Explanation: Once again, the student misunderstands the idiom and, therefore, illogically connects two parts of the sentence.

7 Mistaken identity

a. At first, I raised the shade. Next I opened the window.
First, I raised the shade. Next I opened the window.

Explanation: *At first* indicates a previous time. It is not a number. *First,* however, is an ordinal number and shows position in a series (1, 2, 3, 4).

b. I am used to getting up early, but now I sleep late.
I used to get up early, but now I sleep late.

Explanation: The student may have mistaken *be used to* for *used to.* (Or he or she misunderstands the meaning of *be used to* and illogically connects the idea of getting up early with the idea of sleeping late. See 6.)

Here are some additional corrections your teacher might make:

8 Singular plural

Many interesting things was going on here.
Many interesting things were going on here.

9 Spelling

Keep quite and listen.
Keep quiet and listen.

10+ Add a word

I used/smoke.
I used to smoke.

10− Subtract a word

Your idea makes the sense.
Your idea makes sense.